Integrating Career Development and Mental Health in Counseling

SETH C. W. HAYDEN

American Counseling Association
counseling.org

Copyright © 2025 American Counseling Association. All rights reserved.

American Counseling Association
2461 Eisenhower Avenue, Suite 300
Alexandria, Viriginia 22314

Published in the United States of America

Library of Congress Cataloging-in-Publication Data

Names: Hayden, Seth C. W., author.
Title: Integrating career development and mental health in counseling / Seth C. W. Hayden, PhD.
Description: Alexandria, VA : American Counseling Association, [2025] |Includes bibliographical references and index.
Identifiers: LCCN 2024055347 (print) | LCCN 2024055348 (ebook) | ISBN9781556204203 (paperback) | ISBN 9781394221592 (epub) | ISBN9781394221608 (adobe pdf)
Subjects: LCSH: Vocational guidance. | Mental health counseling. |Counseling. | Career development.
Classification: LCC HF5381 .H3333 2025 (print) | LCC HF5381 (ebook) | DDC650.101/9--dc23/eng/20250128
LC record available at https://lccn.loc.gov/2024055347
LC ebook record available at https://lccn.loc.gov/2024055348

Contents

Acknowledgements vii
1. Relevance of Career Development in Counseling 1
2. Career Development and Mental Health 15
3. Integrated Assessments 31
4. Integrated Career and Mental Health Frameworks 45
5. Marginalized Populations and Career Development 61
6. Integrated Service Delivery and Scope of Practice 79
7. Ethical Dimensions of Career and Mental Health Support ... 93
8. Case Studies 105
9. Future Directions of Integrated Career and Mental
   Health Counseling 113
   References 125
   Index 151

Acknowledgements

To my parents, Bill and Nan Hayden, my sister, Jeny Reinoso, and especially my amazing wife, Jaci, who have encouraged and supported me over the years. To my three girls, Hadley, Eileen, and Lanie, who inspire me to work toward creating a world where they can thrive. To my mentors and colleagues at the University of Memphis, University of Virginia, Florida State University, and Wake Forest University, whose dedication to the counseling profession and counselor education is incredibly inspiring. To Carolyn Baker, Christine Fruin, and Tom Cadorette at the American Counseling Association, whose dedication and hard work were instrumental in the completion of this book.

And to all counselors who tirelessly strive to alleviate suffering and enhance career and mental well-being. Your efforts to support those in need truly make the world a better place.

1

Relevance of Career Development in Counseling

"So, tell me about the binder, " I asked. This statement arose out of curiosity while engaging with someone in a university career center. They came to the university career center for a résumé critique, a reasonably common request in this context. Facilitating a résumé critique is often a relatively straightforward task in which the career practitioner reacts to the information in the document to determine strategies for effectively conveying one's educational and professional background to secure an opportunity or position. This activity occurred frequently in my work in this facility. Given my background as a mental health counselor and my burgeoning interest in the connection between career development and mental health, I tended to consider the broader context of individuals' experiences in relation to career and work regardless of the perceived need (e.g., résumé critique, interviewing skills, negotiating a job offer). Most often, these inquiries would uncover a reasonable response directly connected to their perceived need. In this instance, my mindset of comprehensive analysis got the best of me when viewing their significantly large binder. This statement led us down a path to a significant mental health assessment and referral, which was the protocol within this facility.

I have often reflected on this experience as an example of the connection between career development and mental health. Though this occurred within the context of a career center, the experience of career and personal struggles is not facility-specific. I've had several experiences across various settings (e.g., community agency, hospital, secondary school) in which co-occurring career and personal concerns were presented. My training as a counselor, focused on wellness, created a lens of seeing all aspects of the human experience as interconnected. My work in my doctoral program in a community-facing training clinic focused on career added depth to my awareness of the impact of the interconnection between career and mental health.

As a counselor educator, I have encountered students who demonstrated a rather tepid interest upon their initial exposure to the subject matter of "career." This was, in fact, my own first reaction to the study of the career realm. Like me, however, the students soon realize the salience of this aspect of people's experience upon the commencement of their clinical training. The training of counselors often involves compartmentalizing specific topics within distinct courses, with those specializing in clinical mental health counseling primarily focusing on mental diagnoses and illness, minimizing career as a primary concern.

Events such as the global pandemic, economic downturns, and other societal factors significantly affect people's ability to fully engage in positive career development and mental health. Given the significant impact of these experiences, counselors are well positioned to support those in need in various settings. Being intentional in learning critical elements of providing career and mental health support is essential to holistically addressing complex concerns.

Career is a central feature of the human experience and, therefore, an essential element of professional counseling. The beginning of the counseling profession in the United States is attributed to Frank Parsons and his establishment of a career counseling center in Boston in 1909 (Hartung & Blustein, 2002). Contemporary formulations of wellness, such as the "Indivisible Self" (Myers & Sweeney, 2004), also indicate career as an essential element of wellness.

Career Development in Relation to Prevention and Wellness

The Indivisible Self Evidence-Based Model identifies career as a secondary factor within the primary factor of Creativity (Myers & Sweeney, 2004). The interconnected domains indicate the relationship between different elements of functioning (see Figure 1.1). As one experiences challenges in one area, it will likely contribute to difficulties in other domains. For example, anxiety around making a career decision might contribute to challenges in one's relationships, sleeping patterns, etc. A point of hope for counselors related to this interconnectedness is that receiving positive support with a concern can have positive manifestations across other domains of functioning. This speaks to the importance of offering effective support in multiple areas of an individual's experience. More specifically, research on wellness and career-sustaining behaviors for professional counselors found a link between these variables (Lawson & Myers, 2011), further illustrating the connection between career and wellness.

Figure 1.1
The Indivisible Self Model

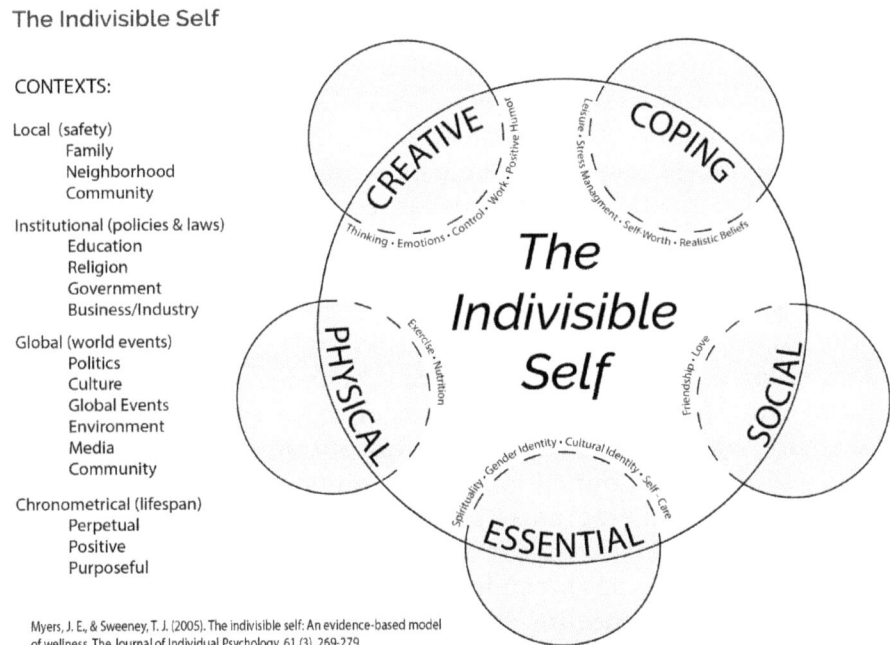

Myers, J. E., & Sweeney, T. J. (2005). The indivisible self: An evidence-based model of wellness. The Journal of Individual Psychology, 61 (3), 269-279.

Researchers have also linked career development with prevention, a primary focus of the counseling profession. The effects of providing effective career support related to mental health and wellness factors can mitigate deleterious outcomes in these domains (Kenny & Di Fabio, 2009). Career development support also has the potential to enhance personal agency by empowering individuals with skills for effective career decision-making and problem-solving (Hayden et al., 2021). Prevention and wellness and their connection to career development offer further evidence of focusing on career development within counseling.

Centrality of Career in the Counseling Profession

Researchers have long considered the relationship between career-focused counseling and traditional psychotherapy (McIlveen, 2015). The connection between mental health and career issues frequently leads mental health-focused counselors to help their clients deal with work satisfaction, underemployment, or unemployment through psychotherapy (Cardoso, 2016).

The definition of counseling, in addition to accreditation standards, specifically identifies career as an essential component of counseling practice. The *20/20: A Vision for the Profession of Counseling* project was a multi-year endeavor to develop a consensus definition of the counseling profession. Through an intensive process that implemented a Delphi method (i.e., input from experts) and consultations with divisions of the American Counseling Association (ACA), the project produced a consensus definition of counseling: "Counseling is a professional relationship that empowers diverse individuals, families, and groups to accomplish mental health, wellness, education, and career goals." (Kaplan et al., 2014). The inclusion of "career" in this definition highlights its importance within a conceptualization of counseling.

The National Career Development Association (NCDA), a division of the American Counseling Association (ACA), predates ACA with its initiation as the National Vocational Guidance Association in 1913 (NCDA, n.d.). This illustrates the long history of career development and counseling within the counseling profession and in the United States.

In addition, the Council for the Accreditation of Counseling and Related Educational Programs (CACREP) accreditation standards have consistently included career development in the foundational counseling curriculum. This has precipitated the provision of a specific career development and counseling course in CACREP-accredited programs of study. The 2024 standards pertaining to career development and counseling include the following: theories and approaches to career development and decision-making (Standard 3.D.1); approaches for conceptualizing the interrelationships among and between work, socioeconomic standing, wellness, disability, trauma, relationships, and other life roles and factors (Standard 3.D.2); developmentally responsive strategies for empowering individuals to engage in culturally sustaining career and educational development and employment opportunities (Standard 3.D.7); and strategies for improving access to educational and occupational opportunities for people from marginalized groups (Standard 3.D.11; CACREP, 2023). The definition of counseling, the inclusion in accreditation standards, and the history of career development in relation to the profession emphasize the importance of this topic within counseling services.

Despite these indicators of this topic's importance within counseling, it is a puzzling reality that students often view career development as less important than other topics within the counseling curriculum. Instructors of the career course indicated the challenge of engaging students in a topic they had little interest in, as well as making the course relevant for them (Osborn & Dames, 2013). In addition, professional school counselors have indicated a lack of confidence in facilitating career readiness in their settings, in both practice and training (Ockerman et al., 2023; Novakovic et al., 2021). Research has indicated that school counselors are more likely to engage in college and career readiness activities when they feel it is important (Novakovic et al., 2021; Anctil et al., 2012), emphasizing the need to elevate career development and counseling within counselor education and training as it impacts the delivery of counseling services.

This creates a unique tension in the preparation of counselors to effectively address career concerns within counseling, as there is a misalignment between the profession and the aspirations of those pursuing careers as counselors. One of the aims of this text is to support those associated with counseling in approaching career concerns both clinically and pedagogically by enhancing their understanding of the complexity of career development, its connection to mental health, and instilling enthusiasm for the subject matter.

Definition of Terms

Before discussing career development and its relevance to counseling, it is important to acknowledge the terminology used to define elements of career development support. There are variations in the specific terms used to describe career services, impacted by history, the context of service delivery, and global elements. Savickas (2003) has spoken at length about the origin of career support in vocational guidance and the evolution of language in describing the iterations of career support. Herr (2013) detailed the history of vocational guidance and its ongoing development in the counseling profession. The following are specific descriptions of various career and vocational support iterations to ensure the reader understands their similarities and differences as we examine career development within counseling. They are listed in alphabetical order for ease of reference.

1. *Career coaching*: Future-focused support involving a more directive approach in which concrete steps are provided for the individual to research and reflect on their careers (indicated by Megan Collins Myers in Lupton-Smith et al., 2024).
2. *Career counseling*: A specialty within the profession of counseling, one that fosters vocational development and work adjustment of individuals at each life stage by engaging them in life planning aimed at the psychosocial integration of individual's abilities, interests, and goals with the work roles structured by the community and occupations organized by companies (Savickas, 2003).
3. *Career development*: Lifelong psychological and behavioral processes and contextual influences shaping one's career over the lifespan (Niles & Karajic, 2008).
4. *Career education*: Refers to the totality of experiences (school-based and otherwise) that help individuals acquire and use the knowledge, skills, and attitudes necessary to make work a meaningful, productive, and satisfying part of life (Rojewski, 2006).
5. *Career guidance*: Supports individuals and groups to discover more about work, leisure, and learning, and to consider their place in the world and plan for their futures (Hooley et al., 2023).
6. *Career planning services*: The active provision of information designed to help clients with specific needs (NCDA, 2015, p. 3).

Other terms, such as vocational education and vocational guidance, have been historically used to support individuals in their career development in various counseling and educational settings. There has been an evolution of vocational guidance to career guidance, with earlier forms focused primarily on supporting adolescents and delivered within schools. Career guidance programs, career counseling, and career services involve consideration of the total spectrum of children and adult populations, including retirees (Herr, 2013). The provided definitions are designed to provide a basic understanding of relevant concepts within career development pertaining to mental health support and the provision of counseling.

Career Counseling and Social Change

The counseling profession has a long history of supporting many diverse populations, many with their own specific concerns. Within the helping professions, counseling possesses a unique origin and identity that impacts several aspects of the profession. Since its initial genesis, counseling has evolved significantly. The focus within clinical and scholarly aspects of the profession has shifted based on prevailing elements within broader society and awareness of dimensions of mental health. The importance of work cannot be understated. A quote from the *In-Work Project,* an endeavor aimed at improving the improving of marginalized populations in the labor market and funded by the European Commission, effectively describes the importance of work:

> It is not only an indispensable means of enhancing individual senses of usefulness and belonging, but also of providing financial means. Work is also central in several other dimensions, namely in its role as a socialising mechanism, as a source of social exchanges, and individual identities. Thus, work can be seen as the pillar of social organisation, but also, to a large extent, as an important pillar of the existential organisation of individuals. It is a fundamental feature in many dimensions of social integration, such as health, housing, and interpersonal networks. (in-work-project.eu, n.d.)

Career development has historically been a touchpoint for awareness and action in social consciousness and mobility. As societies have evolved, the impact of work on people's lives and well-being has had significant implications. Within the United States, notable events have changed and shaped both career and work, which has provided an enhanced understanding of the centrality of work in people's lives. The aforementioned roots of the counseling profession in the United States involved societal advocacy when Frank Parsons conceptualized career development as involving personal factors and focused on social reform for poor immigrants (Stebleton & Eggerth, 2012).

Societies evolve with geographic shifts, technological advancements, and significant events and movements. At the heart of many of these changes is career and work. Advancements for marginalized groups such as women, LGBTQ+, and people of color have been made through occupational access and attainment. Dr. Mark Pope's *Social Transition State Model* (2000) examines the evolution of career and work in the United States. Starting with the 1890s and working up to 2000, he identified various societal events and movements in the U.S. and their implications for career-focused support in service delivery and educational settings. This work contextualizes this ongoing process of social change and how it intersects with career services.

There has been additional consideration of career development and its connection to broader societal events and forces. Hagen and Hagen (1995) examined the profound effects of the Civil Rights Acts of 1965 and 1991, expanding on the application of disparate impact and treatment of employment discrimination. Legislation such as this has often focused on the workplace as a venue for the manifestation of equal treatment under the law.

Alshabani and Soto (2020) have also examined the impact of career counseling for women in the early 20th century and its influence on their mobility within the workplace in the United States. The feminization of careers, variation of support based on racial groups, and focus on providing career support to White, educated, nonimmigrant women have inhibited the development of effective career counseling for women. They recommend future research on career-focused counseling for women of color.

Shen-Miller et al. (2012) outline the historical events concerning career development in the United States (Table 1.1). This organization of career and work in stages indicates a shift in career based on developments and societal events.

Table 1.1

Significant Events in the Development of Career Development in the U.S.

Stage	Timeframe	Notable Events
One	1890–1914	Post-Civil War, Urbanization, Beginning of Vocational Guidance
Two	1914–1929	Focus on Measurement, Vocational Education and Organization, Post-WWI Vocational Support
Three	1929–1939	The Great Depression, Widespread Economic Depression, Vocational Legislation
Four	1940–1957	Post-WWII, Increase in Vocational Instruments, Shift from Vocational Guidance to Career Counseling and Development
Five	1958–1970	Space Race, Increased Focus on Science and Technology, Civil Rights Movement, The Great Society

Stage	Timeframe	Notable Events
Six	1970–1979	Enhance Attention to Career Needs of Ethnic Minorities and People with Disabilities, Career Development Theory Focused on Social Learning
Seven	1980–1989	Second Largest Wave of Immigration, Increase Attention on the Needs of Diverse Populations, Shift to Holistic Models of Career Development
Eight	1990–2005	Enhanced Focus on School-to-Work Transition, Attention to Inclusivity within Career Development Theories, Career Counseling Outcome Research, Rise Postmodern Career Theories
Nine	2005–present	Information Age, Globalization, Automation of Labor, Pandemic, Social Justice Movement, Standards and Credentialing in Career Services

Though a central feature of the human experience, career development is not always fully considered within the counseling profession. One could argue that counseling originated within the context of addressing societal elements of career. The enhanced focus on mental health within counseling is an understandable development, given the evolving societal awareness of mental well-being. This text aspires to step away from the compartmentalization of domains of human functioning to provide evidence for the integration of career development and mental health and the implications of integration for counseling practice, research, and training. The following is information on the history of career-focused counseling and social movements in the U.S. and how career development connects with the primary features of the counseling identity (e.g., wellness, prevention).

Frank Parsons

Frank Parsons's work was instrumental in shaping the counseling profession. Parsons advocated for a systematic approach to understanding oneself and determining the degree to which this knowledge informs vocational choice. From 1906–08, he developed the vocational guidance movement (Jones, 1994). He advocated for using a scientific approach to select a vocation with consideration for a person's aptitudes, abilities, ambitions, resources, and limitations (Parsons, 1909). The creation of the Vocational Bureau of Boston and the establishment of principles that guided vocational guidance were landmark contributions to the field. This expansion of the process of vocational choice, which includes dimensions of self, was instrumental in establishing the profession of counseling (Blustein & Hartung, 2002).

Parsons's approach was instrumental in enacting social change in the realm of work during this time (O'Brien, 2001). The early 20th-century social and political reformation movements possess the possibility of offering a relevant vision for contemporary times by comprehending career decision-making and counseling as a socially situated process entailing purposeful reasoning, prudent intuition, and sustained efforts at ameliorating social injustice (Hershenson, 2008). This legacy of improving societal conditions and enacting interventions designed to enhance an individual's ability to work meaningfully still resonates with the counseling field (O'Brien, 2001).

Parsons's Trait and Factor Theory

Parsons (1909) viewed three primary factors in vocational choice: a) a clear understanding of yourself involving aptitudes, abilities, interests, ambitions, resources, limitations, and their causes; b) knowledge of the requirements and conditions of success related to advantages and disadvantages, compensation, opportunities, and prospects in different lines of work; and c) true reasoning on the association between these two groups of factors. Contemplating the combination of these elements is essential in making the "greatest decision" of one's life (Parsons, 1909, p. 5). The introduction of this framework stimulated research focused on obtaining detailed information about individual differences and methods of assessment (first step), occupations (second step), and the decision-making prospect itself (third step) (Herr, 2013).

This focus on traits and factors that inform the career development process has been a bedrock for career frameworks and theories since its inception (Hartung & Blustein, 2002). Many contemporary theories have stemmed from this approach. Though there is some indication that the concept of trait and factor within vocational guidance predated Parsons (Hershenson, 2008), Parsons's systematization of the approach and identification of specific characteristics, such as the aforementioned primary factors, contributes to the continual attribution of the beginning of vocational guidance to his early conceptualization of career decision making.

More can certainly be said about Parsons's work. There are also several additional iterations of career development and frameworks for support. Subsequent chapters will discuss additional career development theories and relevant factors related to career development. As indicated, this text intends to centralize career development within the counseling profession and enhance the abilities of counselors and those who train them to address the career development concerns of those they serve. Though abstract at times, the information provided is designed to be directly applied in practice and training. The following sections are designed with this aim in mind. *Views from the Field* offers practitioners' perspectives on specific topics within each chapter to provide diverse voices from those in the field operating in various settings. The *Pro Tips for Providers* is designed to offer quick reference tips for consideration for those addressing career-related concerns within counseling. The aim is to focus the information on developing specific interventions to implement within a therapeutic engagement.

The following chapters will expand on what has been identified in this chapter and introduce new elements for consideration. My aspiration for this text is that it will help ensure all counselors consider the connection between career development and mental health in all settings.

Conclusion

Career development and counseling are the foundational focus of the counseling profession. As society has evolved, realizing the importance of work in personal fulfillment and societal advancement has inculcated the intersection of career development and mental health. Counselors with an awareness of the centrality of career development in the human experience are well positioned to offer integrated career and mental health-focused support. The dynamic landscape of career and mental health necessitates an informed and integrated approach in which these topics are addressed simultaneously. Through this lens, individuals can form a framework of counseling in which attention is devoted to both career and mental health concerns and the relationship between these domains.

Pro Tips for Providers

- Become familiar with the history of career in relation to the development of the counseling profession as it contextualizes the unique identity of the counseling profession and its focus within the helping professions.

- Learn the connection between career development and other elements of human functioning via conceptualizations of wellness.
- Consider career development as a means of prevention and ways in which career support can mitigate difficulties in other areas, such as mental health.
- Career development can also be viewed as a means of enhancing agency in relation to career decision-making and problem-solving via skills development.
- Emphasize career development within counseling practice and training as this reflects indicated evidence of the importance of these topics within the experience of those receiving counseling services.

Views from the Field

Amy Willard, MA, NCC
Wake Forest University

Any Willard has over ten years of career development experience working with individuals and groups in the higher education setting. She is currently the Director of Student Career Education and Experience in the Office of Personal Career Development at Wake Forest University, where she serves liberal arts and sciences undergraduate students. She collaborates with academic and campus student engagement partners to integrate career development across campus.

The intersection of career development and mental health is a compelling narrative that unfolds frequently within the university setting. Drawing from my experience as a university career counselor, I witnessed the transformative power that intentional career guidance can have on the mental health of students. Contextual influences, including social, political, and economic factors, shaped career counseling interventions.

These factors affect university students' mental health. This was particularly evident during the COVID-19 pandemic and the years since. University students were grappling with loneliness on full campuses, social/political reckoning nationally, virtual technology fatigue, the loss of internships and jobs, and grieving the loss of loved ones. These instances affected students across colleges and universities nationally, and their well-being suffered.

During the pandemic, my career center's career counselors sent emails to our caseloads offering support for our students beyond career development to mitigate and triage their mental health. One reply I received from a student was noticeably clear. They were suffering from depression after losing a job opportunity that they had worked so diligently to land. The student felt hopeless that no one was in a similar position as them (no internship experience and no job/internship offer) and dwelled on other areas of their life that were not going well. The pandemic compounded these feelings for this student. I shared that many peers experienced similar, if not the same, circumstances—they were not alone. I worked with them to instill hope, focus on their strengths, and receive appropriate services for their underlying symptoms. Symptomatically, what the student was experiencing was beyond the boundaries of competence within my role. Therefore, I referred the student to another university service where the student received proper care.

However, addressing mental health concerns without acknowledging the role of career can leave a critical piece of the puzzle unexplored. As a result, I worked alongside the student "to foster greater self-clarity within [themselves], who then [used their] enhanced self-understanding to identify career options that help translate life experiences into career opportunities" (Amundson et al., 2014, p. 3). This translated to the student switching career paths to positions better aligned with their background, interests, skills, and values. Additionally, I encouraged the student to register for an alumni event to connect with industry professionals. By increasing their self-efficacy, creating attainable goals, and reversing their narrative from a place of deficit to strength, the student landed a full-time position a few months later.

As a career counselor, I utilize essential helping skills to navigate the underlying stress and anxiety expressed through their body language (often not shared verbally) and hold space for students. Oftentimes, they enter the office with a particular career development question(s) to solve but cannot move forward. "The client's presenting issues aren't necessarily the only or most immediate need" (Smith, A. C. & Peterssen, K., 2024, p. 245). Therefore, students bring not only their career aspirations into the room but also their life stories and backgrounds, which can affect their mental health. Recognizing the interconnectedness of these elements allows us to provide more holistic and effective interventions. Redekopp and Huston (2019) state that "In essence, all career development interventions are well-being interventions" (p. 252). Addressing these issues enables students to progress in their career development more effectively. It comes from a place where they increase their mental well-being and focus on their strengths, what is happening now, and what they *can do* to keep advancing toward their goals. In the dynamic landscape of counseling, understanding the centrality of career in the human experience is paramount.

2

Career Development and Mental Health

When teaching career development courses and facilitating training on career service delivery, I often ask the audience to consider their path to their current place in their career and all the factors that have impacted this journey. Invariably, family, finances, identity, meaning, resources, and elements of well-being are indicated. Over the course of several years of asking these questions of different audiences, I have seen similar outcomes occur across various settings, verifying the consistency of experiences. This anecdotal inquiry is valuable in helping the audience understand the importance of career development. This activity invites participants to reflect on impactful events and experiences in their professional progression and uncovers an understood association between the various dimensions of one's life and career development.

My initial interest in this subject matter arose from observing the effects of economic uncertainty on overall well-being. During my doctoral studies, I served as coordinator of the Personal and Career Development Center, a counselor education training clinic at the University of Virginia. Though the clinic served students at the university, members of the surrounding community could also access services from providers in the clinic. This was during 2008–2012, which has come to be known as the "Great Recession" (Duggan, 2023). This systemic event, though more severely impacting those in a lower socioeconomic circumstance per usual during economic downturns, also caused distress for individuals across professions. While providing counseling services, I observed the devastating effects of career and work uncertainty on mental health and well-being, which solidified my desire to further investigate the connection between career development and mental health in both my clinical and scholarly work. Despite the fluctuations in economic conditions, the significant impact of career concerns on individuals has persisted.

Though anecdotal testaments to this connection are illuminating, more definitive scientific information is needed to ensure counselors are aware of specific career development and mental health influencing individuals' experiences. Mental health concerns are the leading cause of work absence due to sickness and long-term disability (Petrie et al., 2018). The current *Diagnostic and Statistical Manual of Mental Disorders*, 5th edition, text revision (DSM-5-TR; American Psychiatric Association, 2022), and previous versions of the manual designate work-related difficulty as an important clinical diagnostic consideration for several psychiatric disorders, such as autism spectrum disorders, bipolar disorder, eating disorders, major depression, and schizophrenia (Dipeolu, Hargrave, & Storlie, 2015). In addition, more holistic approaches to career counseling that include consideration of mental health issues have been emphasized (Blustein, 2008; Hinkelman & Luzzo, 2007; Krumboltz, 1993; Lenz, Peterson, Reardon, & Saunders, 2010; Zunker, 2008).

Societal Trends in Career Development

The experience of individuals and groups within society impacts counseling in several ways. As discussed in Chapter 1, historical events affect the nature of work. A contemporary example is the COVID-19 global pandemic, which began at the end of 2019 and was globally widespread by early 2020. This experience had broad, sweeping implications for people worldwide in almost every sector of work. Though individuals in varying contexts uniquely experienced the impact, it was a significant event that exhibited the connection between career and mental health as well as the fluid nature of work. The work of educators, food and hospitality service workers, and many other professionals dramatically changed very quickly. The implications of these changes permeated several dimensions of people's lives. Adverse circumstances such as the COVID-19 pandemic increased career anxiety (Mahmud, Talukder,

& Rahman, 2021). This event created disruptions in work and the facilitation of career support services (Osborn et al., 2022).

Research also indicates the emergence of artificial intelligence has created an uncertain landscape for people. The American Psychological Association *Work in America Survey* found that 38% of workers in the United States worry that artificial intelligence may make some or all of their job duties obsolete (American Psychological Association, 2023). These are just a few examples of how broader experiences shared by many intersect with career development and, by extension, concerns presented within counseling services.

Further consideration has been given to the nature of work and its impact on individuals. Decent and precarious work, the focus on the worker's experience, and the effect of systematic conditions on their well-being are ongoing topics of focus in career development practice and research (Blustein, 2019; Blustein et al., 2020). The shifting landscape of various jobs and occupations significantly impacts those in the workforce.

The gap between research and practice in counseling requires attention as it limits the capacity for both practitioners and researchers to fully realize the potential of their work. Murray (2009) indicated a chasm between researchers and practitioners, with researchers expressing that practitioners dismiss their work and practitioners indicating that research is inadequate in addressing the needs of their clients. In addition, practitioners in other helping professions shared the main barriers to using research: insufficient facilities, lack of time to read research, and difficulty understanding statistical analyses (Murray, 2009). Though the focus of this text is not specifically on research, it is important to understand the contextual factors that may inhibit the application of career-focused research into practice.

There is a wealth of research on career and mental health constructs based on various conceptualizations of career development. This chapter aims to provide the reader with an overview of this information, enabling them to tailor their work to the needs of those they serve.

Integration of Theory, Research, and Practice

To explore the connection between career development and mental health research, it is necessary to frame the manner in which theory, research, and practice interact with each other. Sampson et al. (2020) offer a conceptualization of connecting these elements.

Figure 2.1

The Theory, Research, and Practice Cycle

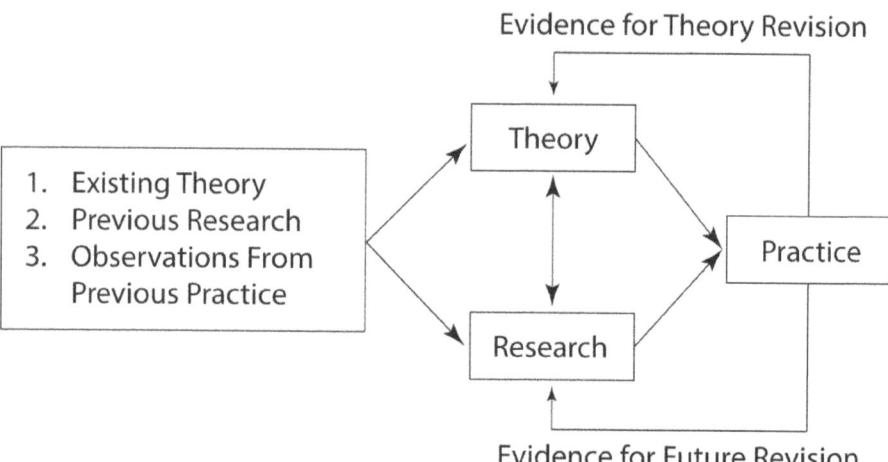

Note. Adapted from "Annual review: A content analysis of career development theory, research, and practice - 2013," by J. P. Sampson et al., 2014, *The Career Development Quarterly, 62*(4), p. 295. Copyright 2014 by the National Career Development Association. Adapted with permission. https://doi.org/10.1002/j.2161-0045.2014.00085.x

Each element is essential to effective counseling practice. As career development is a central feature of human functioning, examining the connection between career development and mental health within counseling is responsive to this reality. While career and mental health are often considered distinct and separate, there is substantial evidence of a connection between these domains. For counselors to effectively address the complex career concerns of those they serve, effective integration of career theory, research, and practice is imperative. With this in mind, the following information examines relevant career development and mental health factors that impact the experience of individuals needing counseling services.

Career Development and Mental Health

There is substantial evidence of the connection between career development and mental health. This information further establishes the connection between these domains and demonstrates a bidirectional relationship between these factors. Redekopp and Huston (2019) indicated the following relationships between work and aspects of mental functioning: (1) work has positive effects on general mental health and well-being; (2) person/work fit is related to mental health and well-being; (3) work-related factors can play a role in the development of mental health concerns; and (4) work-related factors can contribute to the development or maintenance of mental health and well-being, serving as effective adjuncts in the treatment of various mental health concerns. A significant question arises related to the implications of this information on counseling practice. This chapter will discuss particular examples, with more to be shared in subsequent chapters. Cognitive, affective, and dimensions of personality have all been associated with dimensions of career development. The following is specific research identifying the manner in which these dimensions are connected.

Executive Functioning

As indicated by the previously mentioned definition of career development, which involves lifelong psychological and behavioral processes and contextual influences shaping one's career over the lifespan (Niles & Karajic, 2008), one can extrapolate the complex process of navigating career and work. The interaction of these factors contributes to a unique experience for each person. Examining the connection between career development and mental health has yielded several insightful findings. The hope is that this information will enable the reader to better understand the depth of association between career development and mental health and respond in kind in their counseling practice.

Executive functioning is defined as a constellation of top-down mental processes involved in effortful control, including inhibition, working memory, cognitive flexibility, planning, problem-solving, and reasoning (Diamond, 2013). This comprehensive definition highlights the breadth of processes involved in the human experience. Specifically, within career development, these elements are brought together with individuals navigating decisions and experiences that influence this process. Several career-focused theories that include these elements in their framework have acknowledged this. One example is the definition of executive processing offered by Sampson et al. (2023): metacognitive functions, including self-talk (silent observations by individuals of their progress in decision-making that can be perceived as positive or negative), self-awareness (the extent to which individuals are aware of themselves as decision-makers, including the potential impact of self-talk), and monitoring and control (the extent to which individuals can monitor their progress in decision-making and control the effects of negative self-talk). Though more focused on career decision-making and problem-solving than the definition of executive functioning, this conceptualization includes dimensions of mental health as it relates to effective engagement in career development. Hayden et al. (2023) directly connected executive processing with career development, discussing how it intersects with mental health and service provision. Within executive functioning are specific dimensions, such as beliefs, feelings, and thoughts, which various experiences impact.

In an attempt to offer a consumable description of the research on this topic, the relevant factors will be organized into the following categories: affective, cognitive, familial influence, personality factors, and trauma. Due to the inherent interconnectedness of these domains, any attempt to discretely categorize these dimensions is limited by the reality of these experiences. While a thorough critique of this framework is warranted, I aim to provide a survey description of the research on these topics described in this section and its implications for counseling practice and research.

Affective Dimensions

Emotions are a powerful component of human behavior. They can motivate people to engage in various behaviors and are connected to their beliefs about themselves, others, and the world around them. Interestingly, emotional intelligence has been associated with career decision-making (Jiang, 2014; Jiang, 2016), with a causal relationship between emotional intelligence and career adaptability (Parmentier et al., 2019). With this in mind, it is important to determine how affective dimensions relate to other aspects of human experience. Previous research has identified several affective states related to career development.

Anxiety

Anxiety, a common emotion, has been consistently indicated as connected to dimensions of career development. In my own clinical work, encountering someone with a career concern who is highly anxious has been fairly common. The American College Health Association's *National College Health Assessment* (ACHA, 2023) highlights the prevalence of anxiety, identifying it as the primary mental health condition reported by a sample of over 23,000 undergraduate students.

Counselors have several options for addressing anxiety related to career development. Should the focus center on career concerns? Is directly addressing the presented anxiety more effective? Or should both be tackled simultaneously? The answers to these questions significantly influence the therapeutic process. Recognizing how anxiety manifests in career development contexts is crucial for identifying effective intervention strategies. One theme has emerged regarding anxiety and career, which is that the relationship is multifaceted. Anxiety impacts career decision-making and problem-solving, while the inverse has also been indicated. Though anxiety is considered a blanket term for this affective state, research further specifies this state and the degree to which the permutations impact dimensions of career development.

Career anxiety (specific emotion associated with an individual's career situation), state anxiety (situational and transitory), and trait anxiety (dispositional and long-lasting) have all been considered concerning their impact on career development. The breadth of research on anxiety related to career is expansive.

Career exploration has been found to be a mediator between trait anxiety—where anxiety is present regularly—and career decision-making (Park et al., 2017). Interestingly, the impact of trait anxiety on aspects of career decision-making changes over time (Jia et al., 2022; Park et al., 2017).

The literature on career development and mental health shows a significant connection between emotions and thoughts, which has several implications for career decision-making and the role of counselors. In relation to the cognitive functions necessary for career decision-making, trait anxiety, but not career anxiety, is negatively associated with attentional control, a cognitive function utilized in career decision-making (Takil & Sari, 2019). Anxiety has also been indicated as associated with negative career thinking (Osborn et al., 2020; Osborn et al., 2016). Worry, an emotional state associated with anxiety, has also been indicated as connected to dysfunctional career thinking and self-perceived processing skills.

Depression

Depression is another cognitive state associated with career development in several ways. Referring back to the ACHA survey, depression was found to be the second-highest indicated experience among undergraduate college students (ACHA, 2023). Similarly, depression has been indicated by almost a third (29%) of adults in the United States (Gallup, 2023). Counselors, regardless of the environment in which they provide services, will encounter depression within their practice. The prevalence of depression, coupled with the frequency of career decision-making, sparks a consideration of ways in which these two factors are related.

Research bears out that these factors are related in several ways. In a seminal work examining the connection between depression and career indecision, Saunders et al. (2000) found depression as significantly related to career indecision. Additionally, Walker and Peterson's research (2012) found negative career thoughts and career indecision were related to symptoms of depression. The dimension of decision-making confusion was identified as the strongest predictor of depression. In high school-age students, depression was found to be higher in less-decided adolescents, with more-decided individuals having higher levels of affect and a higher sense of well-being (Amaral et al., 2023).

Depression has also been found to be related to dysfunctional career thinking as well as a sense of meaning and purpose in life (Buzzetta et al., 2020). Further, depression is associated with dimensions of negative career thoughts such as decision-making confusion and commitment anxiety (Dieringer et al., 2017). In this same study, negative career thoughts were strongly related to hopelessness, highlighting the magnitude of the impact of career on an individual's perceptions of themselves and the world. The inverse relationship between depression and career decidedness is evidenced in research by Rottinghaus et al. (2009), in which those with clear career goals exhibited fewer symptoms of depression than those with fewer career goals. Hayden et al. (2016) indicated the link between major depressive disorder and career development. Often the work of career exploration involves determining the client's or student's elevated interest in various fields. The diminishment of interest can blunt this process.

Hope

Hope is another affective state indicated as important in decision-making and problem-solving. Hope has been linked with several factors, such as self-efficacy, vocational identity, and career engagement (Amundson et al., 2018). Hope has also been indicated as related to various academic and career activities, such as motivation to interact with instructors, completing assignments, and increasing awareness of personal goals, interests, and values involved in vocational identity development (Smith et al., 2014; Yoon et al., 2015).

The inverse is that hopelessness has been found to be associated with negative career thinking. Decision-making confusion, a facet of negative career thoughts, accounted for significant variance in hopelessness (Dieringer et al., 2017). Hopelessness has also been associated with career barriers for women pursuing leadership roles in the workplace (Türkü Kılavuz & Yusuf İnandı, 2022). Interestingly, the potential adverse effects of unemployment can be mitigated by career-focused counseling as it enhances self-efficacy, promotes social engagement, and bolsters self-concept.

When encountering an extreme state of hopelessness, such as those who are at risk of completing suicide, career-focused support offers a means in which to instill hope. Cureton and Tovey (2023) connected the SHORES model (S - Skills and strategies for coping, H - Hope, O - Objections, R - Reasons to live and restricted means, E - Engaged care, S - Support), a suicide resiliency tool to aspects of career development. Employment instability and its implications can increase the risk of suicide (Howard et al., 2021); examining co-occurring career and mental health concerns through this lens can help instill hope in those struggling with career concerns.

The connection between affective states and career development is substantial. Further research is needed to enhance our understanding of the various affective states. To this point, the focus has been on less favorable emotional states such as anxiety and depression. More is needed to understand emotions, such as excitement, contentment, and the like. The implications of this connection for counselors working with various populations in various settings are essential to consider. Given these connections, developing comprehensive assessment and intervention tools (more on this in later chapters) is imperative.

Cognitive Dimensions

Beliefs, perceptions, and thoughts, categorized as cognitive dimensions, greatly influence the navigation of the career development process. This is an area of significant focus within the career development literature. Various theories and extensive studies have focused on cognitive dimensions related to career and work. The beliefs and views people have about career and work significantly impact their experience, with substantial evidence indicating the connection between cognitive dimensions and career development. Self-efficacy, career thoughts, and various forms of readiness are examples of specific constructs examined at length. Understanding the dimensions of cognitive factors helps inform interventions.

Self-Efficacy

Self-efficacy has been consistently identified as a key factor in career development. In general, *self-efficacy* is defined as "the belief in one's ability to successfully perform a given behavior which is required to produce certain outcomes" (McAuliffe, 1992, p. 26). Career decision self-efficacy was originally defined by Taylor and Betz (1983) as an individual's belief that they can successfully complete tasks related to career decision-making. Specifically, self-efficacy has been indicated as impactful on career choice (Ye, 2014) and decidedness (Restubog et al., 2010).

Considering one's view of their capability to succeed in the process is related to various career development factors. Evidence has consistently demonstrated that self-efficacy is a significant cognitive factor in relation to career dimensions. Several studies have focused on the experience of anxiety with regard to various career factors. Career self-efficacy significantly impacts career exploratory behavior (Sheu, 2023). The interaction among other mental health factors, self-efficacy, career factors, secure attachments, greater perceived social support, and fewer career barriers increased self-efficacy in academic and career domains (Wright et al., 2014). Further, social support, career self-efficacy, and career decision-making have been indicated as related (Jemini-Gashi et al., 2021). Finally, lower career decision-making self-efficacy and higher incidences of negative career thoughts are associated with career decision-making difficulties (Bullock-Yowell et al., 2014).

Extensive research has been conducted on self-efficacy in relation to career development, and more research continues to be undertaken. Social Cognitive Career Theory (SCCT; Lent, 2005; Lent et al., 1994) and the specific component of self-efficacy beliefs have also been extensively researched. Though varying in its relationship with various factors, self-efficacy emerges as impactful within an individual's career development and mental health experience.

Career Thoughts

Beliefs and thoughts are also significant areas of consideration related to the connection between career development and mental health. When considering the tasks associated with career development—exploring options, making a decision, and engaging with others (e.g., interviews, networking, etc.)—it becomes apparent that thoughts will influence this process in various ways. There is a perception that career-focused concerns are resolved through specific activities such as gathering information to enhance understanding of options, improving relevant documents like resumes and curricula vitae, and enhancing marketability through education and training. While these are helpful tasks that can be applied when appropriate, paying attention to the impact of thoughts on the career development process is essential to successfully attaining goals. The connection between thoughts and aspects of career epitomizes the connection between career development and mental health.

The concept of career belief and thoughts has been codified within specific career theories such as cognitive information processing theory (CIP; Sampson et al., 2020; Sampson et al., 2004). Though the categorization involves a tremendous amount of overlap, differentiation of these elements is helpful in offering a framework to better understand the impact of career thinking on career and mental health factors.

Dysfunctional career thoughts within CIP are termed negative career thoughts about one's career (Sampson et al., 2020). Dysfunctional career thoughts have been linked with various adverse outcomes such as anxiety (Bullock-Yowell et al., 2011), career self-efficacy (Bullock-Yowell, Andrews et al., 2011), depression (Dieringer et al., 2017; Saunders et al., 2000; Walker & Peterson, 2012), and vocational identity (Jo et al., 2016). Dysfunctional career thoughts have also been connected to several dimensions of career planning. Career thoughts were found to be a significant factor related to confidence in making a career decision (El-Hassan & Ghalayini, 2020). Evidence consistently indicates the impact of beliefs and thoughts on career and mental health factors.

Familial and Personality Factors

In addition to the affective and cognitive factors associated with elements of career, the influence of caregivers and family has been indicated. Evidence shows that personal, familial, environmental, and systematic factors can impact children's aspirations and preferences for future occupations (Howard et al., 2015). In addition, parental figures appear to strongly influence a child's vocational development (Ginevra et al., 2015). Self-efficacy and the experience of happiness, family influence and support, students' work, and academic satisfaction were indicated as factors influencing these career decisions (Koçak et al., 2021). This demonstrates the importance of familial influence on the connection between career and mental health.

When considering personality factors based on the Five Factor Model of Personality, there are indications of connections with career dimensions. This model indicates a general personality structure consisting of the five broad domains of neuroticism (or emotional instability versus stability), extraversion (versus introversion), openness (or unconventionality), agreeableness (versus antagonism), and conscientiousness (or constraint versus disinhibition) (Costa & McCrae, 2009). Neuroticism, further described as a characteristic in which a person has a general tendency to experience adverse effects—anger, embarrassment, fear, guilt, and disgust—has been found to be associated with negative career thinking and career decision state (Bullock et al., 2015). Furthermore, the combined effects of neuroticism, extraversion, openness, agreeableness, and conscientiousness accounted for significant variance in negative career thinking (Coleman et al., 2023). These familial and personality factors further illustrate the connection between career development and mental health. The implications of these findings are immense for counselors as they expand to relevant considerations in providing career and/or mental health support.

Trauma

Greater attention is being paid to the impact of trauma on people's ability to navigate career development. Adverse childhood experiences have been found to negatively impact career (Powers & Duys, 2020). Currie and Widom (2010) found that those with a history of abuse and neglect have lower levels of education, employment, and earnings. Those with histories of abuse and neglect also have a diminished likelihood of employment in middle age.

In addition, women returning to work who have experienced interpersonal violence have struggled with physical issues, social isolation, loss of control, and feeling disconnected (Ballou et al., 2015). Those receiving treatment for chronic posttraumatic stress disorder experience an impaired ability to perform time management demands, output demands, and mental interpersonal demands at work (Wald, 2009). Interestingly, trauma symptoms along with posttraumatic growth were found to be predictive of career adaptability (Prescod & Zeligman, 2018). These findings situate the experience of trauma with career development.

Conclusion

Research on mental health and career development is robust, offering guidance on the relevant factors worthy of consideration. The curated list of research in this chapter is thorough yet not comprehensive, as the extensive literature on the subject is expansive and continually evolving. Specific journals such as *The Career Development Quarterly, The British Journal of Guidance and Counselling,* the *International Journal for Educational and Vocational Guidance, The Journal of Career Development,* and *The Journal of Vocational Behavior* are but a few of the many journals that contain research on the connection between career development and mental health. The changing conditions in the workforce and the experiences of those we serve require a dynamic response from counselors to effectively respond to this reality. Operating from a lens of integrating career and mental health in practice, research, and theory offers a pathway to effective support.

Pro Tips for Providers

- When considering effective ways to support those struggling with career development and mental health, it is essential to develop your specific awareness of the intersection of these domains is essential.
- Be curious about how these domains are connected in the conceptualization phase of counseling, as this will offer pathways to exploration within counseling to develop integrated interventions.
- Assess identified factors such as career thoughts, decent work, hope, self-efficacy, familial and personality characteristics, and trauma in your counseling practice. This will enable you to address the explicit and implicit dimensions of a concern.
- Actively engage with the professional knowledge base through professional development and examination of literature to stay abreast of developments in the integration of career development and mental health (e.g., the COVID-19 pandemic).

Voices from the Field

Dr. Monica P. Band
Mindful Healing Counseling Services, LLC

In 2023, the career landscape witnessed significant shifts, influenced by various factors impacting employment and the economy. One of the most prominent trends is the continued expansion of remote work. The COVID-19 pandemic accelerated the adoption of remote work, and by 2023, it had become a permanent fixture for many industries. While this offers flexibility, it also blurs the boundaries between work and personal life, contributing to mental health challenges such as burnout and isolation. I currently support clients in an insurance-based private practice setting in an urban city, offering in-person and telehealth appointments.

Similarly, this has created opportunities for many of my clients, particularly women and families with children, to optimize their time, energy, potential, and productivity rather than commute or spend additional money on services to delegate household tasks and childcare. Mental health challenges come with negotiating shifting responsibilities and accessibility to work. Initial conversations in career counseling may first have to do with understanding one's physical environment in how they set up their space, mindfulness capitalizing on the times of days they are more productive, strategies around workflow and time management, and practicing how to say "yes" and "no" as a basis of exercising one's boundaries.

To my clients in their 20s–30s, remote work is seen as a solution to decentering career identity and accessing a balanced personal lifestyle of travel and quality time with loved ones. For example, one of my clients left a government position with a salary and benefits to embrace a nomadic lifestyle, living a few months or less in different states or countries. This career decision comes with worries and concerns, particularly in explaining it to their family members who value security, safety, and a more conventional and risk-averse career path. Career counseling in these cases may include role plays regarding conversations with friends and family members on their decisions, challenging and exploring the anxiety of others not understanding or approving of their career decisions, and reflections on self-efficacy and confidence.

Secondly, the gig economy has grown exponentially, with a surge in freelancers and independent contractors. While this provides individuals with diverse income streams, it often needs more stability and benefits of traditional employment, contributing to financial insecurity and stress. Clients who do gig work can make it more difficult for clients to access mental health services, not having healthcare benefits or a secure income to pay out-of-network expenses. Thankfully, with the trend of AI and social media, there are more resources than ever for people to access to support their mental health. Career counseling may look like psychoeducation around the various uses of assistive technology.

Finally, within my practice, those not seeking gig work and prefer the stability of a conventional career path are looking for value-based, impactful work. In other words, instead of pursuing a field or career incentivized primarily by money or prestige, people seek jobs that align with their values and offer positive social impact. Career exploration looks very different in these cases, focused on identifying how values manifest in our behaviors.

3

Integrated Assessments

Assessments are an essential component of counseling practice. In the counseling world, assessments and various measures are frequently utilized to deliver services. Building off the previous discussion of the connection between career development and mental health, the concept of "integrated assessment" means using both assessments to offer insights into the career and mental health status of those served by the counselor. This information will hopefully inform counseling interventions. One belief I have that other counselors might not share is that assessments are not interventions but are intended to inform next steps in the counseling process.

Career assessments have a long history of utilization and are designed to offer clarity in response to people's uncertainty around current and future occupational options. During my time in a university career center, visitors would come in and ask to "take the test." In fact, clients typically expect psychological tests in career counseling and the counselor's advice on the right career (Cardoso et al., 2012). This clear directive is underlaid with an expectation of what the assessment will provide them. In more mental health-focused environments, engaging with clients around relevant career concerns will often lead to identifying a career assessment to uncover information that will facilitate meeting counseling goals.

This chapter will offer specific information on career and mental health assessments and their relevance in addressing the connection between career and mental health. Within the 2024 CACREP Standards for counseling programs, an understanding of the identification, selection, and administration of counseling assessments (Standard 3.G) has been indicated as necessary for the competent delivery of counseling services. For career development, Standard 3.D.5 calls for "strategies for assessing abilities, interests, values, personality, and other factors contributing to career development" (CACREP, 2024). As values and personality consist of thoughts, feelings, or behaviors, their inclusion in this standard acknowledges the connection between career development and mental health. The other areas of "abilities, interests ... and other factors" are also impacted by aspects of mental health. With this in mind, it is important to identify specific assessment measures and strategies related to counseling practice.

In addition to CACREP standards, the *Diagnostic and Statistical Manual of Mental Disorders* (5th ed.; DSM-5; American Psychiatric Association [APA], 2013) identifies work-related difficulty as an important clinical diagnostic consideration for several psychiatric disorders, such as autism spectrum disorder, bipolar disorder, eating disorders, major depression, and schizophrenia (Dipeolu, Hargrave, & Storlie, 2015). The most recent version of the *Diagnostic and Statistical Manual of Mental Disorders* (*DSM-5-TR*; APA, 2022) considers the impact of symptomatology on occupational functioning and work as part of the diagnostic criteria for various disorders, highlighting the connection between career and mental health.

This translates to other areas of focus within counseling, such as rehabilitation and school counseling, that utilize assessments to gain insight into the experience of those being served. Ensuring competence in understanding the bridge between career development and mental health is essential in holistically addressing the needs of those being served. When assessing various aspects of one's experience, formal and informal means of gathering information are utilized. Regardless of their settings, counselors are tasked with facilitating assessment techniques that effectively identify aspects of people's experiences relevant to the therapeutic engagement.

Numerous counseling assessments exist that may be administered. Assessments uncover relationships between elements of career and mental health, which can then be used to inform interventions. The information is categorized into objective and subjective assessments. Specifically, career services are often characterized by a significant use of career assessments. They are frequently used to address an identified career concern. There is evidence that career-focused assessments are useful in screening for elements of mental health. There are also experiences in mental health that impact career development, as previously indicated in Chapter 2. Integrating career development and mental health via counseling assessments offers a structured approach to evaluating a client's experience and developing comprehensive counseling interventions. Two categories of assessments are objective and subjective measures. The following offers specific information on the assessments and research indicating their utility in determining co-occurring career and mental health concerns and informing counselors' strategies.

Objective Assessments

With regard to objective assessments, several measures include career development and mental health factors. There is evidence that career assessments are a direct bridge to dimensions of mental health. In addition, results from mental health-focused assessments are worthy of consideration concerning career concerns, as this can significantly impact one's experience in career and work. Though the assessments presented here bridge this gap, it is essential to acknowledge the extensive nature and volume of career assessments and their use in counseling. The presented measures are those in which there is evidence of their utility in assessing dimensions of mental health and the structure of the assessment, which indicates dimensions of affective and cognitive functioning.

Career Thoughts Inventory

The *Career Thoughts Inventory* (CTI; Sampson et al., 1996, 1996a) is associated with cognitive information processing theory (Sampson et al., 2023, 2020). It is uniquely structured to identify career development and mental health concerns. The theory, discussed in more detail in Chapter 4, is intended to identify elements of the executive processing domain (i.e., the act of managing and controlling the thoughts, emotions, and activities within and between the components of career problem-solving and decision-making) in the pyramid of information processing (Sampson 2023).

The CTI is a 48-item measure of negative career thinking related to career problem-solving and decision-making. The assessment provides a total score and three subscale scores: Decision-Making Confusion

(DMC), Commitment Anxiety (CA), and External Conflict (EC). The total score indicates the total amount of negative career thinking and one's ability to engage in the career decision-making process. The DMC scale assesses one's inability to start or sustain the career decision-making process due to emotions or lack of understanding. An example item from the DMC subscale is, "I'm so frustrated with the process of choosing a field of study or occupation I just want to forget about it for now." The CA scale indicates one's inability to commit to a choice and generalized anxiety about the outcome. A sample item from the CA subscale is, "I worry a great deal about choosing the right field of study or occupation." The EC scale measures one's inability to separate self-perception from the input of others, which leads to a reluctance to assume responsibility for making a decision. An example item from the EC subscale is, "I'm always getting mixed messages about my career choice from important people in my life." Responses are measured on a 4-point Likert scale ranging from 0 (*strongly disagree*) to 3 (*strongly agree*). The CTI was normed for use with high school juniors and seniors, college students, and adults. This assessment tool helps bridge the gap between career development and mental health. By indicating the dimensions of various scales, such as DMC, CA, and EC, and overall negative career thoughts, counselors working with clients who face career and mental health concerns can use the CTI to learn more about a client's experience in navigating these issues.

Dieringer et al. (2017) found that the elevations on the DMC and CA scales were linked with major depressive disorder indicated on *Beck's Depression Inventory* (version II; Beck et al., 1996), and DMC was also found to be predictive of hopelessness measured by the *Beck Hopelessness Scale* (Beck, 1993). The CTI total score has also been associated with scores on the *Meaning in Life Questionnaire* (MLQ; Steger et al., 2006), especially the "presence of meaning" scale (Buzzetta et al., 2020). These important findings offer a direct connection between career development and mental health.

Counselors using the CTI gain insight into dimensions of executive processing as well as a potential window into mental health factors. Awareness of the assessment and ways to use the results inform both decisions to further assess for mental health concerns and develop comprehensive counseling interventions.

In addition to the assessment, a CTI workbook (Sampson et al., 1996b) is used in conjunction with the measure for the client and counseling to collaboratively address negative career thoughts. This cognitive restructuring exercise helps to replace negative career thoughts with more accurate and functional beliefs that promote positive career development.

Career Decision Self-Efficacy Scale

The *Career Decision Self-Efficacy Scale* (CDSES; Taylor & Betz, 1983) measures career decision-making self-efficacy. This measure assesses self-efficacy as conceptualized by Bandura's social learning theory (1977) and, by extension, in the realm of career decision-making within social cognitive career theory (Lent et al., 1994). The instrument includes five subscales—Gathering Occupational Information, Goal Selection, Plans for Implementation, Problem-Solving, and Self-Appraisal—derived from Crites's (1976) theory of career maturity, with 10 items per subscale.

Career decision-making self-efficacy is indicated as a relevant factor in task completion and engagement in career decision-making. Self-efficacy has been differentiated from overall global self-esteem and is associated with psychological distress and self-esteem, emphasizing the importance of this dimension within career development and mental health (Thompson et al., 2019).

The CDSES short form (CDSE-SF; Betz, Klein, & Taylor, 1996) consists of 25 items and uses a 5-point Likert scale ranging from 1 (*strongly disagree*) to 5 (*strongly agree*). Like the full-length assessment, the short form uses the same five subscales, with five items per subscale. Sample items are "I can choose one job among the jobs I am considering" and "I can tell what the ideal job is for me."

In terms of utilizing the CDSES to bridge the gap between career development and mental health factors, counselors can use this measure to get a sense of one's belief in their ability to complete career-related tasks and the degree that results from this assessment may be a window into other dimensions of mental health. Results from the CDSES can inform counseling interventions and help determine next steps in addressing co-occurring career and mental health concerns.

Career State Inventory

A person's readiness to engage in the process of career decision-making is essential. The readiness component is connected to Cognitive Information Processing (CIP; Sampson et al., 2023, 2020). *Career decision-making readiness* is defined as one's preparation for deliberate and effortful career decision-making and problem-solving (Bullock-Yowell, Saunders, & Peterson, 2015). Several internal and external factors impact one's ability to effectively engage in the process. Many of these factors are mental health-oriented, meaning assessing readiness involves exploring several dimensions of one's experience.

The *Career State Inventory* (CSI; Leierer et al., 2017) is designed to assess an individual's current (state) career decision-making readiness (Leierer et al., 2016). The CSI measures three dimensions of career: certainty, satisfaction, and clarity (Leierer et al., 2017). The assessment uses items from established career-related scales, such as the *Occupational Alternatives Questionnaire* (Slaney, 1978, 1980) for certainty, which asks respondents to think about all the occupations they are considering and indicate their first choice. Satisfaction is measured by the question, "How satisfied are you with your first choice?" Responses are rated on a 5-point Likert-type scale ranging from 1 (*very satisfied*) to 5 (*very dissatisfied*). Vocational clarity is assessed using three true/false items from the *My Vocational Situation* (Holland et al., 1980): "If I had to make an occupational choice right now, I'm afraid I would make a bad choice," "Making up my mind about a career has been a long and difficult problem for me," and "I am confused about the whole problem of deciding on a career."

This measure can be used both as an assessment tool of the current state of one's readiness and as a measure of the impact of counseling interventions on the mental health-oriented dimensions of clarity, satisfaction, and clarity. Though the assessment is inherently focused on career, gaining insight into a client's readiness invites exploration into several aspects of their experience. A counselor's posture of curiosity enables them to key into connected experiences and determine the reciprocal relationship between career and mental health.

Self-Directed Search

John Holland's (1959) theory of career choice, based on the RIASEC model of personality types and work environments—Realistic, Investigative, Artistic, Social, Enterprising, and Conventional—is foundational to the structure of the *Self-Directed Search* (SDS; Holland & Messer, 2017). This assessment involves identifying various components of one's interest and the degree to which these align with characteristics of work environments. The assessment consists of the respondent indicating occupational daydreams, activities, competencies, occupations, and self-estimates of traits. The *Holland Occupational Code* (HOC) is developed from the responses to the items in these assessment sections in which the three components of RIASEC are indicated in the specific order of their magnitude. Corresponding occupational options similarly categorized are then examined to determine potential vocational options.

Integrated Assessments

The Strong Interest Inventory also includes the HOC but presents this information in a much different manner. This method of aligning interests with the work environment has been supported in empirical investigation of this conceptualization of a career choice (Nauta, 2010). In addition, interest fit aligns with job satisfaction and, more specifically, performance outcomes and satisfaction with one's overall career path (Hoff et al., 2020).

This measure also helps explore how one's interests connect to their mental health experience. The Holland Hexagon (Figure 3.1) visually represents relationships among the RIASEC dimensions. When two interest areas, such as Realistic and Investigative, are adjacent, it is easier to identify corresponding career or life options that align with these interests. However, identifying satisfying options becomes more difficult when interest areas are oppositional, such as Realistic and Social. This misalignment can cause frustration for individuals as they navigate a limited range of choices.

Figure 3.1
Holland's RIASEC Hexagon

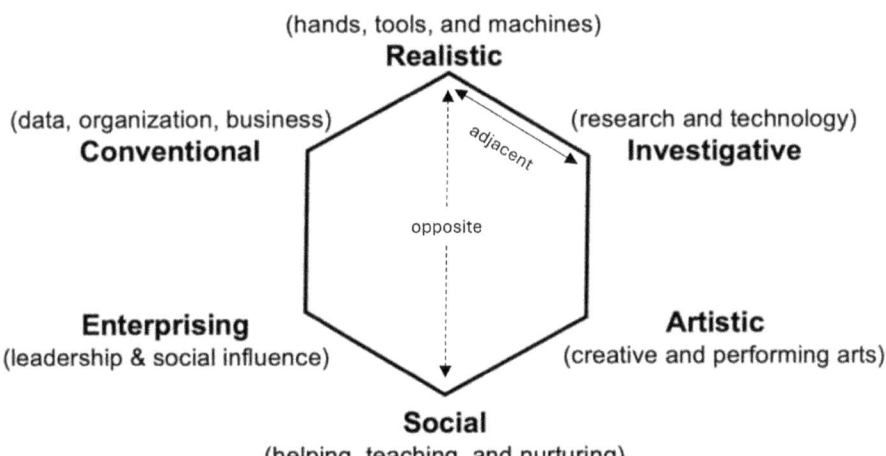

Note. Adapted from *Holland's RIASEC Hexagon: A paradigm for life and work decisions*, by E. Bullock-Yowell and R. C. Reardon, 2024, Florida State Open Publishing. Copyright 2024 by Florida State Open Publishing.

This is but one example of how information from the SDS can be used to uncover characteristics of a person's experience. An expansive description of Holland's model and methods for using this within counseling can be found in *Holland's RIASEC Hexagon: A paradigm for life and work decisions* (Bullock-Yowell & Reardon, 2024). Although primarily focused on career interests, the *Self-Directed Search* offers insight into the broader dimensions of the client's experience. Expanding the use of the assessment in this way can be fruitful in appropriately conceptualizing the indicated concern.

When considering the potential for mental health concerns impacting perceptions and capacity to indicate interests, various mental health diagnoses, such as major depressive disorder (APA, 2022), involve diminished interests. The inverse would be mania associated with bipolar disorder, in which significant elevations of feelings of happiness and euphoria may impact interest in various occupations (APA, 2022). In either instance, the mental health experience can impact career dimensions. When examining results with a client with no significantly low or high-interest levels, a counselor can explore affective and cognitive functioning to determine relevant factors contributing to the results.

Whether utilizing the indicated objective measures or others, considering the manner in which mental health intersects with the factors being assessed is important. In addition to objective assessments, subjective assessments are valuable tools in identifying interrelated career and mental health factors.

Subjective Assessments

Comprehensive Intake Interview

A common practice in the initiation of counseling is completing an intake interview. This process is designed to gather information about a client's experience in various domains such as career/work, education, family, mental health, physical functioning, relationships, and social support. Intake interviews are often conducted by counselors in diverse settings to gather information and form potential diagnostic impressions (Gladding & Newsome, 2018). The intake interview may be structured or less structured depending on various factors related to the setting or preferred manner of facilitation by the counselor.

A point of consideration concerning the intake interview is to gather as much information as possible about the client's experience to obtain a comprehensive picture of their experience. Exploration of aspects of career and work and the occupational experiences of caregivers and family members can provide important information on the relationship between career and mental health. Given that familial and parental influence contribute to career development outcomes (Metheny & McWhirter, 2013; Raymund et al., 2015) and impact affective and cognitive factors, gathering information concerning personal and familial career and work is necessary. One way to contextualize the purpose of exploring these topics is to indicate that this information will enable the counselor to better understand the client's whole experience to better determine areas of potential assets and challenges related to the presenting concern.

Although intake procedures may vary across settings, it is essential to explore career-related aspects in the same way personal and familial mental health history is gathered during the initial counseling session. This integrated approach can provide valuable insights into the interconnected nature of career and mental health experiences.

Decision Space Worksheet

Contextual and personal elements interact in various ways, adding complexity to the counselor's ability to understand the relevant factors that affect a client's experience. The *Decision Space Worksheet* activity is a subjective assessment that captures personal, social, and economic context dimensions impacting a career concern.

The *Decision Space Worksheet* (DSW) activity, focused on understanding clients' career concerns, is a projective assessment that reveals the elements in the personal, social, and economic context of a career problem that clients perceive in the moment (Peterson et al., 2016). The activity is intended to help clients conceptualize, organize, and clarify all the elements associated with their career concern. Completing the DSW enables the client and counselor to gain insight into the elements impacting the client's experience (e.g., thoughts, feelings, relationships, financial aspects).

The activity entails the client listing the relevant elements impacting their career decision. After identifying these elements, the client then engages in a cognitive mapping exercise, which involves the client prioritizing the elements in relation to their relevance and importance to the career concern (Peterson et al., 2016). The final step consists of generating a graphical representation of these elements and the magnitude of their importance and potential connection with each other. The results of this assessment are then processed within the counseling engagement.

As clients often struggle with understanding the various factors that impact their experience, the DSW is useful as an experiential activity to clarify the degree of importance of these factors related to their concern. The collaboration between the client and the counselor in completing this activity can also help enhance the therapeutic relationship.

Card Sorts

An additional subjective assessment that captures the connection between career development and mental health is a card-sorting activity. Card sorts have been used within assistive engagements for a long time, with the first known public mention of the activity occurring at the 1961 American Psychological Association Conference (Osborn et al., 2015). There have since been numerous formal and informal iterations of this activity. Though somewhat transtheoretical, focusing on the client's meaning associated with options aligns with aspects of a constructivist counseling approach (Osborn et al., 2015).

The activity involves classifying options into various categories connected to indicated options. Card sorts could include occupational interests, career values, and other relevant topics. The classification categories could be "most likely," "likely," and "least likely." The cards that are sorted contain specific options with brief descriptions. The client organizes the option cards into the indicated categories. Concerning career and mental health, the process and outcomes reveal the existence and interconnectivity of these factors.

The role of the counselor involves observing the client's completion of the task and processing the outcomes of the categorization process. When a client exhibits uncertainty around the placement of the options card, the counselor can comment on the client's uncertainty to assist them in the task and gain insight into their affective and cognitive experience.

Specific indicators of potential issues with mental health are the client's experience of completing the task and the frequency of categorization of the options cards. If the client struggles with the completion of the task, this could be indicative of mental health factors impacting this process. In addition, if the number of options cards is overly classified in a particular category, such as "most likely" or "least likely," there is a potential window into a connection between career and mental health factors.

Conclusion

Career development and mental health are interrelated elements. Integrated assessments offer a means by which to identify related factors. Objective and subjective assessments provide different means to gain insight into how career development and mental health are being experienced by those receiving services. Although a selected number of assessments were described in how they elicit insight into these related factors, looking for instances in which assessments offer glimpses into career development and mental health that can inform the development of comprehensive support.

> ### Pro Tips for Providers
>
> - View assessments as a gateway to the intersection of career development and mental health as both career- and mental health-focused assessments offer pathways to fully understand the nature of one's experience.
> - Utilize existing assessment tools (e.g., *The Career Thoughts Inventory, The Career Construction Interview, The Beck Depression Inventory*) through the lens of the interconnection between career and mental health. This will inform an integration approach to addressing co-occurring concerns.
> - Facilitate a comprehensive intake assessment in which information on the individual and their families' career and mental health functioning is included to offer context to their experience of career development and mental health.
> - Interpret assessment results through the lens of integrated career and mental health, as this can offer insight into how each domain impacts the other.
> - Utilize assessment results to inform integrated career development and mental health interventions.
> - Receive ongoing training on implementing various assessment tools to address co-occurring career and mental health concerns.

Voices from the Field

Erin Bennett, EdS
Florida State University

Mental Health/Use of Assessments – Strong Interest Inventory

I am a Career Counselor with the NCC credential. My experience has been 10+ years in higher ed state institutions, serving as a career counselor and career coach. My clients have been primarily college-age adults, non-traditional college students, and community members. The demographics of clients I have served in coaching and counseling appointments range across various gender identities and race identities.

One of the assessments I have used the most in my counseling practice is the *Strong Interest Inventory College Profile* (SII). One memorable experience involved working with a college-age student over six weeks during weekly career counseling sessions. I assisted them in using the assessment to help select a major. Upon our first meeting, the student took the SII Assessment, identifying their gender as "female." The client was depressed and anxious about their decision and was seeking career counseling to assist. The student presented as a female at the time and felt pressured to choose this option as the SII was coded as a binary assessment. The results seemed valid in identifying their interests, with a high Conventional and Investigative theme, as the client was also interested in the computer science and biology majors. However, the client repeatedly dismissed the assessment results and did not seek to utilize them in their decision-making as heavily as I had seen in other client sessions. Instead, the client expressed frustration, apathy, and hesitation in applying the suggested occupations to their major and career exploration and their progress toward choosing a major.

Upon our third meeting, the client disclosed that they were in the process of transitioning genders, and they would prefer for me to use the "they/them" pronouns. They eventually aspired to transition to present fully male, and at that time would like to utilize the "he/him" pronouns. Upon this discovery, I invited the client to re-take the SII aligned with their gender. The client was surprised this was an option and was interested to know that it could potentially make a difference in their assessment results.

There were no significant differences in the results upon taking it the second time using the male gender selection. The client still measured high on the Conventional and Investigative themes, with many of the same occupations suggested. However, the client's affect towards the results changed drastically. The client was more interested in exploring and considering the results in their decision-making. I pointed out the lack of difference to the client, but they dismissed this information and aligned themselves with the male-gendered results only. They had an unmistakable sense of empowerment, knowing they could better identify with the normed population for the male-gendered SII assessment. The progress in the client's decision-making towards choosing a major began to trend in a more positive direction, and they became less depressed throughout our counseling relationship as their mental health improved. They were more open to the counseling process once they experienced an assessment tool they trusted. This client case is a memorable example of how important it is to have assessments that clients trust and can incorporate into their belief system. As of May 2023, the Myers-Briggs Company has published the *Strong 244 Career & Interest Assessment*, which includes gender-neutral scoring, a larger sample reference sample, more occupational scores, new basic interest scales, and a new report (Wood, 2023). I am excited that this new version will support gender-inclusivity, allowing clients to see the tool as more valid and trustworthy.

4

Integrated Career and Mental Health Frameworks

Given the previous information regarding the connection between career development and mental health, counseling theories often encapsulate the connection between these domains. In my early experience as a graduate student, the focus on career and mental health as a function of separate courses covering these subjects was indicated as discrete categories within counseling practice. Now, as a counselor educator, I have come to understand the organization of a counseling curriculum and aligning student learning outcomes with accreditation standards. For organizational purposes, having discrete courses for the various areas of counselor training offers a workable structure for matching course content, learning objectives, and accreditation standards. Creating separation between these subjects is not representative of the integration of career development and mental health factors within the lived experience of those receiving services. One area in which these domains of functioning are connected is counseling theories.

A *counseling theory* is an intellectual model that purports certain ideas about underlying factors that affect behavior, thoughts, emotions, interpersonal interactions, or interpretations (Cottone, 2017). Interestingly, behaviors, thoughts, emotions, interpersonal interactions, and interpersonal interpretations embody career development and mental health aspects. The "underlying factors" indicated in Cottone's definition encompass those related to career and mental health dimensions. These factors can impact mental well-being, which in turn can impact career development.

In counseling training, counseling and career theories are often presented separately. While career and counseling theories have distinctive characteristics, several connections exist between these frameworks. An example of this connection is found in the cognitive-behavioral foundations of Social Cognitive Career Theory (Lent et al., 1994; Lent & Brown, 2008) and Cognitive Information Processing Theory (Sampson et al., 2023).

The following information will discuss various theories that speak to both career and mental health dimensions to further expand understanding of the relationship between career and mental health elements. This information is not comprehensive, and other resources are available to fully immerse oneself in career development theories (e.g., Niles & Harris-Bowlsbey, 2022). This discussion aims to connect career development and mental health within selected counseling and career theories that encapsulate theory, research, and practice integration. The overarching focus on the evidence within the framework of an intersection of career development and mental health has influenced the selection of these approaches.

Dimensions of Mental Health

As discussed in Chapter 2, the interconnected dimensions of career and mental health add some complexity to the work of a counselor tasked with supporting people navigating these issues. Various common mental health concerns such as Generalized Anxiety Disorder and Major Depressive Disorder (American Psychiatric Association [APA], 2022) may arise or be exacerbated by experiences with career and work. This relationship is bidirectional, as difficulties in career and work can contribute to the development of mental health concerns. This intersection is firmly established, requiring counselors to utilize comprehensive and holistic approaches to support.

Various counseling theories focus primarily on aspects of mental health, with an acknowledgment of the potential impact of multiple factors on career development and occupational functioning, both in assessment and practice. Specific career theories seem to include the interconnected dimensions of career development and work, which is not to say that counselors who operate purely from a traditional counseling theory do not integrate a focus on career and work as many do. Determining theories that, at their core, represent an evidence-based understanding of the interaction of career and mental health factors, the selected theories for this discussion are designed with an acknowledgment of the intersection of career development and mental health represented in their composition.

Foundational Theories

Several theories, including Parsons's framework (Parsons, 1909) and Super's Life-Span, Life-Space Theory (Super, 1990; D. Super, Savickas, & C. Super, 1996), incorporate dimensions of mental health into their theoretical conceptualizations. Parsons's concept of knowing about one's self (i.e., aptitudes, abilities, interests, resources, limitations, and other qualities), developing knowledge of the requirements and conditions of success, and using "true reasoning" to consider these two sets of facts includes several dimensions of mental health.

In addition, Super's conceptualization of career development consists of a segmented framework of other theories, including several developmental and relational elements acknowledging people's various roles and experiences. It emphasizes *self-concept* as a "picture of the self in some role, situation, or position, performing some set of functions, or in some web of relationships" (Super, 1963, p. 18).

Another approach that builds off Bandura's social learning theory (Bandura, 1986) is Krumboltz's social learning theory of career counseling (Krumboltz et al., 1976). Similar to Super's approach, this theory includes career development and mental health dimensions. This approach focuses on four specific factors that influence career decision-making: a) genetic endowment and special abilities, b) environmental conditions and events, c) learning experiences (i.e., instrumental learning experiences and associative learning experiences), and d) task approach skills (e.g., work habits, cognitive and perceptual processes, mental sets, emotional responses). The interaction among these variables impacts one's career decision-making.

John Holland's Theory of Types and Person-Environment Interactions

Holland's approach, which consists of individual differences in personality types and the determination of fit within occupational environments, lends itself to dimensions of mental health that influence this typology. As discussed in Chapter 3, Holland's theory of career choice involves the RIASEC (i.e., Realistic, Investigative, Artistic, Social, Enterprising, and Conventional) model of personality types and work environment (Holland, 1959).

Utilizing the elements of Parsons's (1909) "true reasoning," a person weighs these inputs to determine appropriate options that align with their interests. Mental health dimensions often emerge when personality types are considered and assessed. When one has diminished or overly elevated interests, which may result from various mental health factors, this may cue a counselor to explore the mental health factors, such as cognitive and affective functioning, beyond the presenting concern. This shows at least one way Holland's framework can elicit elements of career development and mental health in its structure.

These approaches have significantly contributed to our understanding of the comprehensive nature of career development and paved the way for additional comprehensive frameworks that include career and mental health dimensions. These theories are often used in conjunction with each other depending on the preferences of the practitioner and the needs of those they serve. The presentation of specific frameworks with regard to their etiology in counseling theories further illustrates the interrelationship between counseling and career-focused theories.

Similar to previous chapters, the selected theories seem to appropriately illustrate career development and mental health integration. The hope is that this will enable counselors to consider the information and determine how career and mental health are included in their chosen theory or approach to counseling services. The section will be organized by the manner in which the theories are grounded in counseling frameworks.

Cognitive Theories

Cognitive behavioral therapy (CBT) is one of the most widely researched and utilized approaches in counseling (APA, n.d.). CBT has been shown to be effective with a wide range of mental health concerns and is based on the premises that 1) mental health concerns are based, in part, on faulty or unhelpful ways of thinking, 2) mental health concerns are based, in part, on learned patterns of unhelpful behavior, and 3) people dealing with issues of mental health can relieve their concerns by learning better ways of coping with them, thereby relieving their symptoms and becoming more effective in their lives (APA, n.d.). From these basic tenets, interventions are developed to address the faulty cognitions that impact behaviors and improve functioning.

Within the realm of career development theory, CBT has significantly influenced the structure of various frameworks. Cognitive Information Processing Theory and Social Cognitive Career Theory are two heavily researched approaches that have emerged from the CBT framework and encapsulate the connection between career development and mental health.

Cognitive Information Processing Theory

Cognitive information processing theory, as discussed in Chapter 3, includes dimensions of mental health, particularly in the executive process domain within the pyramid of information processing, the CASVE (Communication, Analysis, Synthesis, Valuing, and Execution) cycle, and the readiness model. Cognitive Information Processing Theory (CIP; Sampson 2023) encompasses both affective and cognitive dimensions within the structure of the career theory. CIP components of the Pyramid of Information Processing, the CASVE cycle, and the readiness for career decision-making and problem-solving model identify specific affective and cognitive factors and how they intersect with navigating a career problem. CIP theory consists of particular elements that comprise career decision-making and problem-solving: the Pyramid of Information Processing containing three domains of information for effective career problem-solving and decision-making (i.e., knowledge, decision-making, executive processing), the CASVE cycle, and the readiness for career decision-making and problem-solving model to determine the level of readiness in two specific areas (i.e., capability, complexity) which informs the degree of support provided by the practitioner. Effective career problem-solving and decision-making involve combining these elements of what one needs to know (Pyramid of Information Processing) and what one needs to do (the CASVE cycle).

Especially within the CIP framework, the executive processing domain is an essential feature that directly connects mental health elements with dimensions of career. Executive processing consists of three metacognitive areas: self-awareness, self-talk, and monitoring and control. These elements interact with other framework dimensions, such as the CASVE cycle.

An additional dimension of executive processing and the theory as a whole is the acknowledgment that life experiences and cultural identity impact the development of the pyramid components and, in turn, influence how individuals understand and apply these components to the career decision-making process (Sampson et al., 2023). Access to resources, cultural identity, personal identity, spiritual affiliations, socioeconomic status, experiences with discrimination, and other factors influence how individuals view and approach problems and make decisions (Autin et al., 2018; Conkel-Ziebell et al., 2019). CIP theory explicitly acknowledges the importance of considering one's culture, personal identity, support network, and other factors (Sampson et al., 2023). These elements are exhibited in the Valuing phase of the CASVE cycle while also permeating all components of the decision-making process and the entirety of the CIP Pyramid.

CIP focuses on the learning engagement between the client/student and practitioner in which enhanced ways of thinking about the career concern can be generalized to other decisions going forward (Sampson et al., 2023). The approach is shared within the helping engagement to enhance agency within the context of career development (Hayden et al., 2021). CIP-based manualized interventions have been found to lessen psychological distress, further supporting the impact of career-focused support on dimensions of mental health (Arifoulline et al., 2024). CIP and its components encompass several dimensions of mental health related to career development.

Social Cognitive Career Theory

Social Cognitive Career Theory (SCCT; Lent et al., 1994) is a well-researched career theory that contains cognitive behavioral theory and Bandura's social learning theory (1986). Adopted from Bandura's triadic reciprocal causation framework, which emphasizes an "expanded range of contextual, person, and behavior factors" (Lent & Brown, 2019, p. 1), SCCT comprises person inputs, contextual affordances, sociocognitive variables and how they affect the formation of vocational interests, career goals, and actions. Notably, self-efficacy beliefs, personal goals, and outcome expectations are components of the approach that impact career development.

Self-efficacy beliefs are indicated as judgments of one's capability to organize and execute courses of action required to perform successfully. Outcome expectations are beliefs about what the results of engaging in specific behaviors will be. Personal goals relate to an individual's determination to engage in certain activities to produce a particular outcome (Bandura, 1986). These elements interact to create various experiences for individuals. Several elements of mental health are inherent in the elements of SCCT.

SCCT-based support is characterized by focusing on these elements (self-efficacy beliefs, outcome expectations, and personal goals) and determining the degree of work needed to modify specific traits hindering progress toward goals. Issues arise when individuals prematurely foreclose on options due to faulty self-efficacy beliefs and/or outcome expectations and/or when individuals do not consider occupational options due to their perception of insurmountable barriers. Addressing faulty self-efficacy beliefs, examining prematurely foreclosed options, and identifying and developing a plan for overcoming perceived barriers and obstacles to goals characterize the work of a career practitioner operating from this approach.

While cognitive-based theories offer frameworks that capture the connection between career development and mental health, other theories within the career realm have been influenced by postmodern approaches. The following describes some of those approaches that encapsulate related career and mental health factors in their conceptualization.

Postmodern Approaches

Postmodern counseling theories posit that reality cannot be discovered but is instead a human construction (Hansen, 2006). From a postmodern viewpoint, a singular truth does not exist within phenomena waiting to be revealed by dispassionate investigators, positing that observers always infuse phenomena with meaning (Hansen, 2006). There has been an increased interest in postmodern perspectives within counseling, specifically career counseling theory, in response to a perceived shift in career and work conditions. Committing to an occupational choice is difficult due to a lack of stability in social structures (Busacca & Rehfuss, 2017).

With this in mind, various postmodern career approaches have emerged, seeking to expand the focus of career development. Various approaches fall within this category, including dimensions of career development and mental health. Postmodern conceptualizations posit careers as being constructed as individuals make choices that express their self-concepts, constructed through the specific experiences they have experienced in multiple environments. People's self-concepts are potentially altered by new experiences and observing the behaviors of others. Their interests are not fixed, and the self is continuously reconstituted (Savickas et al., 2009). With this in mind, various approaches emerge that focus on constructivist and nonlinear approaches to career development.

Career Construction and Life Design Frameworks

The Career Construction and Life Design frameworks align with a constructivist approach, emphasizing how individuals actively develop meaning in relation to various aspects of career development. Underlying this approach are five presuppositions, which include dimensions of mental health. First, there is a shift in Life Design career support from state and trait indicated in other theories to context (Savickas et al., 2009). Second, there is a shift in focus from content and information to process—one specific quote embodies this premise: "Counselors must discuss 'how to do' not 'what to do.'" (Savickas et al., p. 242). Third, Life Design posits that the focus of career support is related to focusing on nonlinear dynamics, with counselors developing iterative strategies for problem-solving. Fourth, developing an understanding of narrative realities with an acknowledgment of people's construction and re-construction of subjective and multiple realities underlies this approach. Fifth and finally, models of variables are developed based on the manner in which they forecast probable outcomes.

Career construction counseling is an interpersonal process that helps individuals create career narratives connecting their self-concepts to work roles, integrating work into their broader lives, and finding meaning through work (Savickas, 2011). This approach highlights the intersection of career development and mental health, incorporating beliefs, experiences, and other psychological factors.

The work of a counselor from this approach entails exploring the client's narrative via tools such as the career construction interview (CCI; Savickas, 2011). The CCI is comprised of six questions designed to elicit responses on the following dimensions: *act* (counseling goals), *actor* (personality, self, or social reputation), *agent* (manifest interests), *author* (script for linking self to setting), *advice* (guidance to self), and *arc* (central problem or preoccupation) (Hartung, 2015). This information informs the counselor of the perspectives that impact career development. Ongoing engagement in these specific areas and assisting the individual being served with reauthoring their story are the aims of this approach.

Chaos Theory

Another postmodern framework for career development that includes dimensions of mental health is the Chaos Theory of Career (CTC; Pryor & Bright, 2011). This conceptualization of career development borrows concepts developed within the humanities and later adopted by psychology to explain how people solve problems (Pryor & Bright). In this framework, reality consists of complex dynamical systems in which there is a continual interplay of influences of stability and change (Pryor & Bright).

The Chaos Theory of Career has four components: *complexity, change, chance,* and *construction*. In relation to *complexity,* CTC posits several contextual factors (e.g., climate, cultural traditions, gender, labor market, media, sexual orientation, politics, health) that can influence career in unpredictable ways (Pryor & Bright, 2011). The construct of *change* refers to the dynamic, interactive, and adaptive nature of human functioning in the world and in making career decisions and taking career action (Pryor & Bright, 2003a, 2003b). *Chance* pertains to unplanned and unpredictable events and experiences that are often crucial and sometimes determinative in the narrative of people's careers (Pryor & Bright, 2003a, 2003b). *Construction* is the lack of ultimate control or predictability that allows individuals to become active participants in creating their futures rather than pawns in a rigidly deterministic system of cause and effect (Pryor & Bright).

Through these constructs, additional concepts are introduced, such as *attractors* (i.e., limitations within systems), *fractals* (emergent systemic patterns over time), *nonlinearity* (i.e., small changes in complex dynamical systems that have the potential to result in disproportionate changes in other parts of the system), *emergence* (i.e., identification of patterns from the functioning of complex dynamical systems across time and different contexts), and *phase shifts* (i.e., when a system's configuration radically alters either quickly or slowly, as in career discontinuities occasioned by unplanned events affecting an individual's career) (Pryor & Bright, 2011).

The Chaos Theory of Career posits that these elements need enhanced emphasis in relation to other theories, given their impact on career development. The theory is considered a reasonable alternative to the earlier discussed trait-matching theory with more lasting effects (McKay, Bright, & Pryor, 2005). Its focus on systems created by interactions between variables in career decision-making, the sensitivity to change within these systems, the role of chance events, and the agency of individuals to shape their futures in light of this unpredictability positions dimensions of mental health as primary within this approach. Though chaos is in the name of the approach, the counselor's work is intentional in assisting the individual in need of identifying the aforementioned elements and determining supportive ways to respond to these occurrences concerning career development.

Other Theories That Include Career Development and Mental Health

The following contemporary approaches also include dimensions of career development and mental health. They consider affective, cognitive, and contextual factors that impact career development. Though their anchoring in existing counseling theory is not as evident as the approaches already covered in this chapter, their inclusion of career development and mental health dimensions warrant discussion.

Happenstance Career Theory

Krumboltz (2009) extended his work in social learning career theory by focusing on aspects of learning that influence career development. Happenstance Learning Theory (HLT) focuses on events in one's life through the perspective of learning and gaining insight. With respect to career counseling, there are several fundamental propositions put forward within this approach: 1) the goal of career counseling is to help clients learn to take actions to achieve more satisfying career and personal lives—not to make a single career decision, 2) career assessments are used to stimulate learning, not to match personal characteristics with occupational characteristics, 3) clients learn to engage in exploratory actions as a way of generating beneficial unplanned events, and 4) the success of counseling is assessed by what the client accomplishes in the real world outside the counseling session. With these ideas in mind, a counselor works with an individual to accept unplanned events and view them through the lens of opportunities to inform career decision-making.

Counselors who operate from this approach focus on orienting clients' expectations toward seeing unplanned occurrences as a normal and necessary component of career development. Second, the presenting concern is used as a starting point to identify what would make the client's life more satisfying. Third, using the client's past experiences as a basis for current action, the goal of empowering clients to view their past successes contains lessons for current actions. Fourth, a counselor sensitizes clients to recognize potential opportunities in which unplanned events can be seen as career opportunities. Finally, counselors work with clients to overcome blocks to action, helping them overcome dysfunctional beliefs that hinder constructive action.

Counselors operating from this approach attend to career and mental health factors to address a client's co-occurring concerns. Career counseling through an HLT approach provides a tangible framework for the client to encounter unexpected events and nonlinearity in life experiences as opportunities for development and growth.

Hope-Action Career Theory

As indicated in the name of this approach, Hope-Action Theory (HAT) positions hope as central to career development. The theory comprises the following competencies: *self-reflection* (i.e., moments when people ask themselves questions about significant life issues), *self-clarity* (i.e., getting to know oneself involves a more in-depth exploration of skills, interests, values, and personality), *visioning* (i.e., actions in this realm are directed toward looking ahead at various possibilities), *goal setting and planning* (i.e., once a person has identified a career direction, it is time to thoughtfully create specific goals and strategies), and *implementation and adapting* (i.e., recognition that things might not work out as planned, requiring modification) (Amundson et al., 2018). Environmental and contextual factors can hinder or support positive career development (Nile et al., 2014). A visual graphic of a pinwheel with hope at the center (Figure 4.1) illustrates the non-sequential influence of these factors and the degree to which environmental factors can influence the factors (Niles et al., 2014).

Several interventions can be derived from the components of this approach. *Walking the problem* involves clients seeing themselves as "walking" toward their desired goals and looking back to where they came from (self-reflection, visioning, and goal setting). *Story Wheels* is used to encourage clients to use storytelling to identify their strengths and assets (self-clarity) (Amundson et al., 2018). *Career Flow* involves imagery of water pathways to understand career development (self-reflection, visioning) (Niles, Amundson, & Neault, 2011). These are examples of the interventions possible through the *Hope-Centered Career Inventory*. It is an instrument that assesses the theory's dimensions and offers an overview of the career development process (Niles, Yoon, & Amundson, 2010). The emphasis on hope, self-reflection, and visioning in the Hope-Action Career Theory highlights key dimensions of this approach, demonstrating its relevance to both career development and mental health.

Figure 4.1

Note. Niles, S. G., In, H., & Amundson, N. E. (2014). Using an action oriented, hope-centered model of career development. *Journal of Asia Pacific Counseling, 4*, 1–13. Image retrieved from Hope-Action Group. (n.d.). *Hope-Action Theory.* https://hope-action.com/

Psychology of Working Theory

The Psychology of Working Theory (PWT; Duffy, Blustein, Diemer, & Austin, 2016) includes career development and mental health as it positions the context of work and the concept of decent work as central to understanding the experience of career and work. The concept of decent work includes: 1) reasonable compensation, 2) access to health care, 3) interpersonally and physically safe working conditions, 4) fair working hours that allow for rest and free time, and 5) organizational values that support familial and social priorities (Duffy et al., 2016; Kaufmann, 2008). The following four factors are moderating predictors of paths to decent work: proactive personality, critical consciousness, social support, and economic conditions (Duffy et al., 2019). In the research on the PWT framework, associations were found between mental health and career and work factors of economic constraints, financial deprivation, and poverty wage employment (Duffy et al., 2019). These associations further emphasize the importance of considering the contextual factors contributing to worker well-being.

As indicated in the approach, the interaction between individuals and the occupational context in relation to securing decent work involves several dimensions of mental health, such as a sense of safety, adequate rest and free time, and familial and social values. A counselor operating from this framework would explore with clients how economic constraint barriers reduce one's sense of choice in occupational decision-making to create a more realistic appraisal of the client's context, alleviating self-blame and enhancing agency (Duffy et al., 2019). In addition, the PWT considers the degree to which discrimination impacts individuals as well as the lack of access to decent work for racial and ethnic minorities. These elements comprise the application of PWT in counseling practice.

Conclusion

The approaches, frameworks, and theories described in this chapter were chosen to illustrate how career development and mental health dimensions are inherent within their structures. Integrating practice, research, and theory in response to the evidence indicating the connection between career development and mental health enables counselors to holistically support their clients. Implementing their use provides a gateway for a counselor to comprehensively conceptualize an individual's concern in order to identify the connection between career and mental health factors. In doing so, the counselor can offer a sophisticated response to complex and interconnected concerns.

Pro Tips for Providers

- Examine counseling approaches and frameworks that integrate career development and mental health in their structures and associated interventions.
- Identify elements of counseling approaches in which career development is tied to aspects of mental health.

- Integrate counseling theory, practice, and research to address integrated career and mental health dimensions.
- Maintain awareness of the body of theoretically informed research that connects career and mental health factors to stay abreast of ongoing developments in counseling theory (e.g., CIP-focused research on negative career thoughts and depression).
- Systematically evaluate counseling services to determine the impact of theoretically grounded interventions on career developme nt and mental health dimensions.
- Regularly attend professional development events and access resources related to theory to stay informed of effective approaches to addressing career and mental health in counseling practice.

Views from the Field

Anna Clara Blesso, MA
Director of Graduate Career & Professional Development, University of Connecticut School of Business

As a career counselor specializing in higher education, it is a significant understatement to convey that the Chaos Theory of Career profoundly informs my interactions with clients. Working closely with a team of highly trained career development professionals, I strive each day to empower clients in their career journey. Specializing in the graduate business population, my work varies tremendously from day to day, from counseling a student who just recently completed their undergraduate degree and has limited professional experience to engaging with another who has decades of expertise but now wishes to pivot into a new industry.

Inclusive of nearly all professional backgrounds, demographic information, lived experiences, and even academic pursuits, a common thread in the student/client experience is the realization that certainty about their career progression and future opportunities is relatively impossible. This development is especially true in a post-COVID landscape, during which layoffs, remote employment, health-related challenges, and an increased desire for work/life balance became the norm.

Through it all, clients often have a common craving to pursue a clear and defined goal post-graduation that presents as a very specific job at a specific target company, which may not always be readily available, accessible, or even the ideal goal after additional reflection and education. In working with clients, several techniques have proven increasingly valuable in recent years:

- *Transitioning concrete, immovable goals into more flexible, shorter-term aspirations.* In working with clients, I first build space to learn more about their specific goals – determining their motivations, world views and lived experience that might impact their career decision-making. Without being discouraging, I help clients focus on flexible, targeted, short-term goals to both help build self-efficacy and increase the opportunity for the unknown.
- *Increasing self-awareness and purposefully building on skill set instead of specific outcomes.* Much of my time spent with clients is grounded in increasing self-awareness, often focused on assessing skill set and executive presence, which then translates to areas of growth for the future. By focusing our time on skills, needs, and areas of growth, as opposed to concrete and specific goals, clients can gain broader experiences and focus away from one specific outcome towards the potential for many, many more.
- *Modeling flexibility and offering a wide array of engagement opportunities.* Especially in our post-pandemic world of work, clients will inevitably face rejection, frustration, and negative responses. With that, as career counselors,

it becomes even more of our goal to model flexible thinking while acknowledging our clients' career trauma and disappointment. Although techniques can vary based on individual need, when a client experiences a blocking event (i.e., a job rejection or less-than-ideal interview performance), I purposefully create a space for them to process the experience while encouraging them to focus on the next steps.

In my genuine experience, career counseling is mental health counseling. Although we each enter the profession with unique viewpoints, I carry the mindset daily that "Who we are at work is who we are in the world." The world calls us to embrace the unknown, to increase self-awareness, and to exist in community. Career counseling is certainly no exception.

5

Marginalized Populations and Career Development

As noted before, dimensions of career development impact people from all backgrounds and identities in all places. I have been fortunate to provide career services in higher education settings committed to serving the broader communities in which they are located. This allowed me access to various populations not traditionally served in higher education settings. One experience that stands out was when I served as a program director of career advising at counseling in a large university career center. This facility allowed community members to request workshops on various topics such as job interviewing, negotiating job offers, and job search strategies. One request I received involved providing a job search strategies workshop to those living in subsidized housing in the community. Though I was curious about how I would share the information and how it would be received, I decided to fulfill this request. I was struck by the degree of enthusiasm the participants had for the content I presented and the complexity of their experience navigating the process of securing decent employment. My awareness of factors contributing to the marginalization of various populations, as it involves career and work, was significantly enhanced. No other experience would have provided this degree of awareness of the importance of career support and the differing positionality of people based on various factors in the process of career development.

In addition, through my involvement in professional organizations such as the National Career Development Association, I have connected with others around the globe regarding aspects of career development. Though there has been significant variation related to career and work in different localities, common factors that constitute the marginalization of diverse groups have been consistently indicated. Volition in career and work selection is impacted to varying degrees by life circumstances, such as the availability of resources, incomes, and race/ethnicity (Blustein, 2006). While the importance of acknowledging marginalization in all instances everywhere cannot be stressed enough, the scope of this chapter focuses on the marginalized groups within the United States, as counselors in this context are the primary audience for this text.

As discussed in Chapter 1, with regard to movements for equity and social justice, career development is replete with oppression and limitations on agency concerning individuals' ability to attain their desired goals. This chapter aims to consider the experience of these different populations from a career development and mental health perspective and how counselors can generally support marginalized populations with co-occurring concerns.

The Codes of Ethics for the American Counseling Association and the National Career Development Association emphasize the importance of diversity, equity, and inclusion regarding aspects of identity (American Counseling Association, 2014; National Career Development Association, 2024). Therefore, counseling practitioners need to understand the diverse experiences of people within our society regarding career development and mental health.

Though various identities are identified and discussed within career and mental health support, it is recognized that intersectional identities can both help and hinder one's well-being. People live multiple, layered identities regarding history, social relations, and the operations of power structures (Symington, 2004). Though still emerging in the knowledge base, attention has been paid to dimensions of intersectionality related to career development (Kang et al., 2015; Sparks, 2017; Wright & Chan, 2022). This attention exemplifies the complexity of the human experience, which manifests itself in career development and mental health. By acknowledging this reality of people's lived experience and identities, examining the characteristics of marginalized populations related to career development can enhance awareness of relevant factors that need attention within counseling.

Counseling as a Scarce Resource

A reality of the societal need for counseling and access to services is primary when discussing ways in which to address the needs of marginalized groups. An awareness of the experience that various populations have regarding career development and mental health is helpful only if paired with a focus on the equitable distribution of services. Sampson et al. (2011) have spoken about striking a balance between access and effectiveness of career services, which extends to broader counseling services. Addressing the needs of marginalized populations must be coupled with a consideration of their access to supportive services.

An argument can be made that a systemic approach is necessary, given that much of the distress experienced by marginalized populations is attributable to the broader context in which they function (Sampson et al., 2011). Considering these factors entails shaping the delivery of services with this in mind. Well-intentioned professional counselors with knowledge of the unique experiences of marginalized individuals should also consider elements of their practice that either enhance or hinder access to services for those most in need. The need for quality counseling services far outstrips our capacity to fill it. Sharing services with this in mind adheres to principles of access, equity, and social justice and requires attention in both career services and public policy when it comes to the allocation of resources for quality career support (Blustein, 2006; Sampson et al., 2011).

Within the following sections, a variety of populations will be discussed, specifically regarding the experience of career development and mental health. The focus will be on their experience and indicated interventions within the literature that benefit members of these populations. As discussed earlier, the intersection of career practice, research, and theory is examined in relation to factors influencing career development and mental health. Though volumes could be written about each of the identified populations concerning their experience of career development and mental health, this chapter aims to provide commentary on the experience of these populations as seen through this integrated lens. The intent is not to minimize their experience but to draw attention to the needs of these populations in hopes of adding to the discourse of effective ways to address the career development and mental health needs of marginalized populations. A more developed resource for providing quality career development support for these populations, *Equity-based Career Development and Postsecondary Transitions: An American Imperative* (Hines & Owens, 2022) is a comprehensive compendium of information. In addition, Chan et al. (2022) also applied relational-cultural theory to career development and relationships, emphasizing that positive and negative social interactions significantly influence mental health and well-being. They also highlighted the role of social justice in fostering authenticity and promoting mental health. This perspective underscores the need to move beyond individual-level considerations and address the contextual, systemic, and interpersonal factors that influence career development and mental health. This text, however, will focus specifically on the relationship between career development and mental health within the populations identified earlier.

BIPOC Communities

As with any community, it is essential to view members of various populations as diverse and wide-ranging in beliefs, identities, and worldviews. The following information focuses on career development and mental health factors indicated within career practice, research, and theory as impacting individuals who comprise the BIPOC population (Black, Indigenous, and People of Color; Merriam-Webster, n.d.). As career development spans the length of one's life (Super, 1980; 1996), experiences at various points in the life cycle, such as discrimination, prejudice, and marginalization, can severely impact the connection between career development and mental health.

Relevant Factors

The experience of marginalized populations often involves persistent messages that impact their view of themselves in the context of others and the world. This continual messaging can influence their self-efficacy. A study by Luzzo and McWhirter (2001) found that students of color had lower self-efficacy for coping with career-related barriers than White students. This disadvantages students of color who face increased barriers and a perception of being unable to cope with these obstacles (Rutledge & Gnilka, 2022). Specifically, girls of color face "double jeopardy" in encountering both racial and gender discrimination, which impacts their career decision self-efficacy and decision-making (Rutledge & Gnilka).

In addition to personal characteristics, there are contextual factors that appear to impact career development and mental health. Regarding youths in low-income, ethnic minority populations, school belonging was found to directly affect vocational hope, while parental involvement and vocational hope were mediated by personal control (Vera et al., 2018). Research also indicates that African Americans make accommodations in the job search process due to discrimination (Pager & Bedulla, 2015).

Racism and ethnic identity have been found to impact career development within the BIPOC community. Within the context of low ethnic identity (connection to aspects of an ethnic group, such as expectations, meaning, and social activities), an increase in racism-related stress was associated with a decrease in career aspirations. Interestingly, there are enhanced career aspirations when increased racism-related stress occurs within the context of high ethnic identity development (Tovar-Murray et al., 2012).

Integrated Interventions

A culturally responsive group career intervention has been found to positively affect career development in student engagement, school engagement, and perceived career barriers (Rutledge & Gnilka, 2022). In addition, research indicates that work facilitates identity development concerning future plans, interests, and values (Thouin et al., 2023). In addition, in working with Latina/o clients, counselors need to consider the presenting concern from the perspective of the client and their culture, which may include the perspectives of the family, extended family, and relevant parties such as those within their community (Flores et al., 2010).

Flores et al. (2010) discussed using a *Cultural Formulation Approach* (CFA; Leong et al., 2007) in working with Latina/o populations of Mexican descent. The discussion of providing support is characterized by the following dimensions developed from CFA: (a) self and cultural identity, (b) self and cultural conception of career problem, (c) self in cultural context, (d) cultural dynamics in the therapeutic relationship, and (e) overall cultural assessment of career counseling interventions. Inherent in this approach is acknowledging the mental health experience of navigating the cultural dimensions of a career concern. Cultural awareness when working with Latina/o clients should address concerns within their cultural context and include perspectives from invested parties, such as family, friends, teachers, and the community (Flores et al., 2010). Though more research exists concerning specific career and mental health support considerations, other overarching considerations emerge. First, evaluating the cultural identity of those being served is primary when working with all people, especially those who identify as a member of the BIPOC community. This experience has been indicated as impacting both past and present career and mental health dimensions. Second, formulating a response based on this information and adapting interventions accordingly is necessary to ensure their needs are being met. Third, it is crucial to be aware of the bias both on the part of the practitioner and in the various elements of career and mental health support, such as theory, assessments, and interventions. Developing an individualized approach informed by the circumstances and characteristics of the client or student is key in providing comprehensive and culturally responsive support that integrates career development in mental health.

LGBTQ+ Populations

In addition to ethnic and racial identity, gender and sexual identity impacts career development and mental health. When considering the societal gendering of work over time, the intersection of societal expectations related to work and its implications for members of the LGBTQ+ community is significant. Like any minoritized group, there is a wide range of experiences to consider. That being said, unique experiences and elements of identity warrant attention within the context of connecting career development and mental health.

Relevant Factors

Members of the LGBTQ+ community encounter several factors that impact career and mental health. As we consider the career development path, LGBTQ+ students do not generally regard educational environments as safe (Yoon et al., 2022). Students who identify as LGBTQ+ struggle to balance their sexual identity with career prospects and decision-making (Chen & Keats, 2016). At a young age, LGBTQ+ students are often victimized due to their identity, which affects their ability to determine viable career options. In addition, those who are struggling to overcome identity confusion also struggle with their self-concept, which has a bearing on their ability to simultaneously engage in career planning. Occupational stereotypes based on gender identity and sexual orientation are likely to impact perceptions of their freedom to choose their career path. Counselors may reinforce these gender-based stereotypes due to their lack of awareness of social biases (Yoon et al.)

Factors such as lack of mentorship/sponsorship, workplace discrimination, bias in hiring and promotion, fear of being out, and lack of inclusive policies and benefits have been identified as barriers to career advancement for LGBTQ+ populations (Ivanovic, 2023). Sexual minority women are affected by the degree of support they receive in their career development. Negative sexual identity is impactful on the level of family career support and career aspirations (Fisher et al., 2011). These factors can significantly impact both career development and mental health factors and speak to the internal and external factors that inhibit career development of this population.

Current research on integrated career and mental health interventions for this population includes the developmental aspects of gender and sexual identity, skewing the research toward self-identification and support for young people. Research of LGB adolescents by Schmidt and Nilsson (2006) supported the *bottleneck hypothesis* (Hetherington, 1991), indicating that young LGB individuals expend psychological energy on navigating the reality of marginalization due to sexual identity, therefore missing key career development activities and tasks. Counselors in various environments will encounter these concerns for LGBTQ+ students. Interventions that account for these factors are essential in providing culturally responsive career development support.

Integrated Interventions

Various interventions are outlined here, including adaptations for this population's specific needs. Counselors who encounter career development concerns related to LGBTQ+ communities need to have an awareness of and appropriately address issues such as the coming out process, cultural and familial values, experience with minoritized status, self-esteem, and identity stability (Datti, 2009). As with much of what has been discussed in this section, more effort is needed to develop and implement interventions for LGBTQ+ individuals. As with any consideration of best practices to support a particular population, it is essential to consider how the individual filters their experience into aspects of career development. With regard to counseling this population, the Association for Lesbian, Gay, Bisexual, and Transgender Issues in Counseling Competencies for Counseling has outlined competencies designed to inform counselors of ways in which to effectively serve this population (ALGBTIC LGBQQIA Competencies Taskforce, 2013).

Given the experience of those with varying gender and sexual identities, offering both systemic and individualized support is key. In addition, the context of the support (e.g., agency, community, school) will also influence how a counselor offers support. For example, there is evidence within STEM fields that LGBT+ students are more likely to be interested in studying STEM courses (38.5% vs. 18.5%) in college if courses in high school contain LGBT+ content (Kosciw et al., 2014). While counselors in school settings are not generally tasked with developing the academic curriculum, advocating to those considering integrating this content can be impactful.

School counselors can offer a variety of responsive services to this population. Examples include career role models, guest speakers, and mentors who can both share their experience and guide LGBTQ+ students through the career development process. In addition, supporting LGBT+ youth in schools through curricular inclusion can open up new career possibilities (Kosciw et al., 2014).

Individuals Within Rural Communities

A population identified as underserved are those who live in rural communities. Approximately one-fifth of the population of the United States live in rural communities (U.S. Census Bureau, 2016). There is an identified disparity between access to services for adults living in rural areas receiving mental health services less frequently and from providers with less specialized training than providers in urban communities (Morales et al., 2020).

Relevant Factors

In terms of educational and career attainment, there are mixed results related to the nature of their experience. While there are indications of scoring better with their non-rural peers on various indicators such as the Nation's Report Card (NAEP; Showalter et al., 2019), those in rural communities also delay beginning higher education or vocational training programs, while postsecondary program completion rates for rural students track below non-rural counterparts (Byun et al., 2015; Koricich et al., 2018). As with any population, there is a within-group variation in various characteristics, such as performance on the NAEP, which in the case of rural communities is impacted by the difference between those in poverty and those who are not (Showalter, 2019). This variation indicates the importance of awareness on the part of counselors supporting this population of the specific experience of those in rural communities to get a clear sense of their experience with career, education, and mental health outcomes.

Integrated Interventions

Gibbons et al. (2019) make a compelling case for the distinct culture and cultural norms that may contribute to their experience. Framing the rural community as a distinct culture that prioritizes assessing its strengths and values before addressing individual career needs creates a unique opportunity for engagement. Bronfenbrenner's Ecological Model (1979) considers the interaction between the individual and the environment (e.g., schools, individuals, parents, etc.). The model posits a series of interconnected systems: the *microsystem* (e.g., work, school, friends, peers, family); the *mesosystem* (interaction between microsystem elements, e.g., peers and family); the *exosystem* (e.g., community resources, mass media, governmental policies); the *macrosystem* (e.g., cultural identity, ideologies, and social conditions, and the *chronosystem* (e.g., environment changes and historical events). This model provides a deep context useful in addressing the career needs of those in rural communities. Though this framework has various applications for different communities, it is particularly relevant to rural communities (Gibbons et al.).

Stoltz et al. (2011) describe facilitating a career intervention with students in a rural school community with a sample of mostly African American students. The participants were assessed on aspects of career adaptability and provided with the assessment results to inform subsequent work in two career counseling sessions. Interestingly, this research points to the importance of assessing aspects of career adaptability as there is variation of outcomes based on these elements. The intervention positively impacted career indecision, demonstrating its usefulness for career development.

A systematic review of well-being and employment interventions for rural and Indigenous populations in Australia indicated reciprocity between these dimensions (Luke et al., 2024). The findings highlighted the importance of developing interventions that accounted for the relationship between well-being and employment, emphasizing social connectedness and self-determination. These findings are consistent with other research on the importance of considering the contextual factors within rural communities that influence career development and mental health.

Neurodivergent Individuals

An emerging awareness of the experience of neurodivergence individuals both in mental health and career development highlights the unique experience of this population. When considering career, neurodivergence refers to a natural range of brain functioning in the workplace based on alternative thinking styles, which includes but is not limited to attention-deficit/hyperactivity disorder (ADHD), autism, dyspraxia, and dyslexia (Szulc et al., 2021). Neurodivergent individuals comprise about 22% of the population (Doyle, 2020). Neurodivergence is a broad conceptualization, but specific mental health experiences, such as attention deficit disorder (ADD) and autism spectrum disorder (ASD), are germane to this discussion due to their mental health characteristics associated with dimensions of career development and work. This population experiences marginalization in the workplace due to a lack of understanding of the benefits they offer when included in work and in facing the challenges they encounter. Neurodivergent individuals should be afforded equal opportunities to participate in work (Coffey & Lovegrove, 2023). There has been a shift in thinking in the way in which neurodivergent individuals, such as those with ASD, are viewed with a movement towards affirming their unique abilities and contributions within the workplace as opposed to limitations of symptoms associated with the diagnosis (Bruyère & Collela, 2022).

Relevant Factors

As previously noted, neurodivergence is a broad category that categorizes individuals within the broader population. With this in mind, the unique characteristics of those with ADHD, ASD, dyspraxia, and the like are worthy of consideration in career development and mental health.

Neurodivergent individuals often have specific communication needs and preferences, sensory sensitivity, and unique executive functioning, all of which significantly impact their work experience (Szulc et al., 2023). Eighty-five percent of college graduates on the autism spectrum are underemployed or unemployed (Pesce, 2019). The research by Pesce shows that the characteristics of various categories within the broader classification of neurodivergence impact career development and mental health.

A key factor contributing to the indicated challenges is that the job search process involves socialization and communication, which puts those with ASD at a disadvantage (Pesce, 2019). In addition, though remote work has been a part of the workplace for many years, the significant shift to this modality of work prompted by the COVID-19 pandemic has drawn attention to unique considerations for this population, especially those concerning communication practices and navigating tensions between productivity and well-being (Das et al.,

2021). Overall levels of well-being of neurodivergent individuals in the workforce are indicated as low, requiring specific attention and support (McDowall et al., 2023).

With regard to helping, there is a lack of assessment instruments that exhibit adequate predictive validity for neurodivergent individuals such as those with ASD (Murray et al., 2016). This paucity of applicable resources creates further marginalization for this population when it comes to counseling support that integrates career development and mental health concerns.

Integrated Interventions

As with all those receiving counseling services, individualizing support to account for the unique experience of individuals is imperative when offering holistic support. Specific to those who are neurodivergent, this customization is especially important due to the complexity of their experience with career, executive functioning, and mental health. While there has been a shift to affirming the unique strengths of neurodivergent individuals, the context of career and work still presents challenges for seeking and successfully engaging in work. These challenges can exacerbate mental health concerns, creating additional stress for neurodivergent individuals with achieving success.

Wong et al. (2020) found that supporting youth on the autism spectrum in achieving career success hinges on empowerment, social skill development, a supportive environment, and cooperative parents. In addition, being creative, knowing the individual, facilitating learning through experiences, working with the community, and teamwork are essential among school personnel tasked with assisting students on the autism spectrum in achieving employment success. This can be applied to counselors working in a variety of settings tasked with supporting youth considered to be neurodivergent.

Within the workplace, factors contributing to successful employment for individuals on the autism spectrum include knowledge and understanding of ASD, the work environment (being supportive), and job matching (aligning work roles with interests, skills, and strengths) (Dreaver et al., 2020). Counselors are well positioned to explore clients' interests, skills, and strengths, advocate for support within their environment, and educate employers on their unique needs. When working with individuals with learning disabilities, particularly those who are in college, various effective interventions have been identified. Instilling hope, encouraging the individual to become educated on the diagnosis, considering the impact of various occupational choices on their mental health experience, helping set realistic goals, reframing cognitive beliefs related to their disability, and building resilience have been found to be useful (Dipeolu, 2011).

Counselors working with neurodivergent individuals should consider the intersection of career development and mental health in terms of the impact of both their specific concern about aspects of career development and the stress associated with engaging in career development from a marginalized position. Counselors need to be trained to address the particular characteristics of individuals with varying degrees of ability through evidence-based interventions tailored to the individuals' interests, needs, and readiness for change (McDowell et al., 2022). Addressing the needs of the individual while focusing on advocacy is key to effective support of neurodivergent individuals.

Intersectional Identities and Career Development

While much of the focus of this chapter has been on the needs of specific marginalized populations, the experience of career development and mental health is also strongly influenced by the intersection of diverse identities. Varying levels of ability, neurodivergence, and gender and racial identities converge to shape an individual's educational, career, and work experience. Understanding how elements converge can significantly influence how individuals experience and benefit from career development and the facilitation of counseling services designed to support them. Intersectionality examines how multiple identities converge to shape an individual's experience and marginalization, such as being female, from a minority ethnic/racial group, and identifying as LGBTQ+. These intersecting identities lead to unique experiences of oppression and trauma distinct from those of the dominant group (Crenshaw, 2005). While research on identity's role in the connection between career development and mental health is limited, empirical evidence and counseling practices addressing intersectionality are even scarcer. Intersectional identities can also impact individuals' views of themselves regarding various disciplines, which translates to aspects of career development. Byars-Winston and Rogers (2019) examined the application of Social Cognitive Career Theory (SCCT; Lent et al., 1994) with intersectional identities of gender, race, self-efficacy beliefs, outcome expectations, and science, i.e., one's professional identity within scientific culture comprised of one's self-recognition and the recognition of a person as a potential scientist (Carlone & Johnson, 2007). Differences were found both in racial (i.e., Black, Hispanic, Latina/o) and gender (i.e., male, female) individuals concerning research career intentions. As these fields are seen as crucial to the advancement of society, consideration of the influence of career development and mental health factors related to intersectional identities is warranted.

Integrated Interventions

There has been some discussion about the intersection of identities in the context of career development and mental health. Wright and Chan (2022) discussed the impact of COVID-19 on marginalized populations and the use of intersectionality theory to address oppression within a school counseling context. Though this focuses primarily on COVID-19's impact, various points can be extrapolated to career development and mental health. Counselors addressing intersectionality within the population they serve need to a) reflect on their own privilege, b) embrace multiple dimensions and interconnectivity across social identities of this population, and c) accentuate the multi-layered forms of oppression experienced by those with intersectional marginalized identities.

Career counselors should be versed in the four experiential sources related to self-efficacy, i.e., personal performance accomplishments (e.g., past successes, mastery experiences), vicarious learning (e.g., observing the explicit behaviors, modeling), socially persuasive communication (e.g., verbal encouragement), and affective arousal experienced while completing a task (e.g., joy or anxiety related to task performance when supporting multiply marginalized individuals (Bandura, 1977).

Conclusion

Marginalized populations have a diverse constellation of considerations related to their career development and mental health. Any effort to fully explain their experience will lack totality and risk oversimplifying their experience. The importance of amplifying these populations' unique career development and mental health needs merits examination. The impact of marginalization has impacts on both career and mental health dimensions, requiring counselors to simultaneously attend to these elements in counseling. Further consideration of how counseling practice, research, and theory of effective interventions serve marginalized populations is needed.

Pro Tips for Providers

- Acknowledge the inherent marginalization of various populations concerning career development and its impact on mental health is essential when working with diverse populations.

- Reflect on one's own positionality in relation to career and work in society to identify potential implicit biases regarding views of successful career development and the experiences of marginalized populations.

- Learn contextual and societal factors that impact populations with regard to career development to account for influence on career development and mental health in the provision of counseling services.

- Examine counseling professional literature to keep informed of research within various populations to inform integrated interventions.

- Advocate for traditionally underrepresented populations associated with career and work to eliminate and minimize obstacles to positive career development and personal well-being.

Views from the Field

Felix Morton IV, PhD, LCMHC (NC), NCC
Assistant Professor, Clinical Mental Health Counseling, Capella University

A great deal of research has contributed to the rapid changes in how professionals understand their career journeys and overall career development. In recent years, more attention has focused on the complex harmony of career attainment and individual mental health and well-being. The role of counselors in career-related therapy has traditionally focused on helping individuals explore their beliefs, values, and skills as it relates to career pursuits, with the hope of helping them make more informed decisions about their ideal career journey. However, when integrating cultural awareness into career counseling, it can be argued that when working with marginalized and historically unrepresented clients, there are deeper considerations counselors must be prepared to explore and process with their clients.

Early in their training, counselors learn the skill of broaching and its vitality in the counseling relationship. *Broaching* is defined as "the counselor's ability to consider how sociopolitical factors such as race influence the client's counseling concerns" (Day-Vines et al., 2016). Broaching helps counselors identify cultural characteristics of clients and themselves that may in some way influence the counseling relationship and then intentionally discuss them with the client. Through my work with marginalized clients and their career experiences, I have found that broaching has become an even more important skill needed to truly understand the complexities of marginalized clients' career experiences. By integrating mental health considerations within career-focused therapy with marginalized clients, broaching has led to greater exploration of three key topics that significantly influence their career decisions, transitions, and, ultimately, development across the lifespan. These topics include a) career stress and burnout driven by cultural motivations, b) identity issues from navigating personal and career contexts, and c) stress and pressure to support a family in need.

Career Stress and Burnout Related to Culturally Driven Motivations

People determine their career aspirations with specific goals in mind. Many of these goals and motivations could be internally or externally driven. Broaching with marginalized folx can reveal identity-aligned drivers in their career pursuits, such as the influence of race, gender, sexual orientation, and other personal characteristics. These identities often shape folx's career choices due to factors like underrepresentation in desired fields or being the first in their families or communities to achieve a particular career milestone. So, while stress and burnout remain an important conversation within the mental health counseling and career context from the perspective of day-to-day individual functioning, it is also extremely important to discuss how these play into the career decision-making process for marginalized clients as they relate to their diverse cultural identities.

Identity-Focused Issues From Cycling Between Personal and Career Contexts

In the mental health field, there has been ongoing discussion and advocacy for the idea of "work-life balance" as it relates to juggling the competing demands and desires of work and our lives outside of work. However, more discussion on the depth of that balance is needed, specifically focused on who we are at work versus at home. Similar to the idea of cultural considerations in the decision-making of marginalized clients, counselors should also consider how this conflict may arise in how our clients "show up" in these competing spaces. Many employers outwardly uplift a dedication to diversity, equity, inclusion, authenticity, and accessibility. However, do many employees feel comfortable showing up as their authentic selves in the workplace? This conflict creates a deeper identity issue for marginalized clients and further creates a division between who they feel like they are and how they must show up at work versus who they can be at home. Much more work and research is needed to better understand this idea of living multiple realities for marginalized clients, both across external contexts and across intersecting identities that they may hold.

Feelings of Stress, Strain, and Pressure to Support Family in Need

Lastly, considerations for work with marginalized clients may also involve a moral commitment and dedication toward service and support of family and care providers. Much of this stress and added pressure stems from historical systems of oppression rooted in our career and education foundations in our society, as well as psychologically and emotionally ingrained in our histories as people. Examples of these mental health considerations in career work may include first-generation college students making career choices based on their abilities to support their families, individuals working multiple jobs to support blended-family households, or high schoolers enlisting in the military with hopes of guaranteed benefits with their families in mind.

While it can be argued that numerous cultural factors can influence an individual's career choices and decisions across their lifespan, these example topic areas demonstrate the need for more conversation and training around the integration of mental health and wellness considerations in career development and counseling with marginalized and historically underrepresented people. Our work as counselors is complex, and it is vital that we work to amplify the unique considerations of the holistic experiences of our clients across the intersection of their identities and lived experiences.

Integrated Service Delivery and Scope of Practice

Within the field of counseling, there are many ways in which counselors support those in need. From various professional settings, populations, and topics, counselors actively address a wide variety of issues pertaining to personal challenges. In my own work, I have provided counseling in a diverse array of settings. While the focus of the place of work impacts the proportion of topics presented, there are significant commonalities related to the client's experiences across areas of their lives. During my internship experience in my master's degree counseling program at a community agency focused on domestic violence, I encountered people struggling with a range of concerns, including the impact of unemployment and underemployment. While working in a university career center, those seeking support shared about their challenges with relationships and mental health challenges such as anxiety and depression, coupled with varying degrees of awareness of the impact of these experiences on their academic and career goals. In my ongoing work with military veterans experiencing homelessness, the connection between career development and mental health often manifests in the stress associated with transitioning out of the military to issues associated with military service, such as traumatic brain injury or posttraumatic stress disorder that can significantly impact career development and occupational attainment. One particular instance involved a participant in a career development group composed of military veterans who discussed ways in which substance use impacted their ability to secure stable employment. The interaction between career development and mental health emerges regardless of the setting in which counseling services are provided.

With that in mind, questions come to light around the integration of counseling services and counselors' scope of practice. In what manner and to what extent are career and mental health challenges addressed within counseling? As I have straddled the worlds of career and mental health environments and encountered people who operate in these spaces, these questions consistently arise. Given the indicated connection between career and mental health and the segmentation of counseling services, a tension exists in which counselors are given a false choice of delineating between career and mental health in their practice. In reality, career and mental health are inextricably linked within holistic counseling support (Tang et al., 2021).

The American Counseling Association Code of Ethics states, "Counselors practice only within the boundaries of their competence, based on their education, training, supervised experience, state and national professional credentials, and appropriate professional experience" (ACA, 2014, Section C.2.a). Counselors who operate in either career- or mental health-focused environments must determine how this connection between the two is appropriately addressed within their scope of practice. Many factors influence this reality, such as organizational policies and procedures, the availability of resources, and the complexity of the concern.

Though the lines separating career development and mental health experiences are not always well-defined, counselors need to be aware of how they can operate appropriately within their scope of practice. The following are considerations designed to inform one's awareness of dimensions of practice, focusing on elements of service provision, such as assessment, intervention, and referral, which will offer concrete ways to determine one's integration of career development and mental health.

Assessment

Assessments within counseling are an area in which scope of practice comes to light. With the abundance of instruments that assess dimensions of these domains, determining their appropriate use in relation to scope of practice is essential. As discussed in Chapter 3, a bridge between career and mental health is illuminated through counseling assessments. Counselors operating in career, mental health, school, and rehabilitation spaces may utilize various assessments to ascertain aspects of an individual's experience.

This documented association between career development and mental health within the realm of assessments (see Dieringer et al., 2017; Dipeolu et al., 2015) raises the question of appropriate facilitation of assessment. Counselors who provide services in various settings will have access to different instruments that may be useful in informing their understanding of the client's experience.

I acknowledge that my training and licensure in clinical mental health counseling influence my perception of the use of assessments to determine the link between career and mental health factors. Operating in both career-focused and mental health settings has allowed me to observe how assessments typically utilized in either setting illuminate awareness of concern in each domain.

The *Standards for Educational and Psychological Testing* published by the American Educational Research Association (AERA), American Psychological Association (APA), and the National Council on Measurement in Education (NCME) indicate that practitioners only use assessments in which they have the appropriate training and expertise (Pearson, n.d.). There are also specific qualifications required to purchase certain instruments, e.g., Levels A, B, and C. Ranging from Level A assessments, which do not require additional training to purchase and administer, to Level C, which requires a high level of training in test interpretation evidenced by a doctoral degree in education- and mental health-related fields, these standards put offer guidance into the variation of expertise needed to utilize various assessments when investigating the connection between career and mental health factors. Counselors selecting various instruments that account for the bridge between career development and mental health must determine their qualifications for administration of assessments.

Specific to administration, use, and interpretation of assessments, the ACA Code of Ethics (2014; Standard E.2.a) indicates, "Counselors use only those testing and assessment services for which they have been trained and are competent." The National Career Development Association Code of Ethics (2024) indicates a similar standard of practice related to the use of assessments to measure the dimensions of career and mental health factors. This mandate requires practitioners to fully consider the nature of their competence to operate within their scope of practice as it pertains to using assessment instruments to evaluate the relationship between dimensions of career and mental health.

In general, career assessments tend to be more accessible, with mental health assessments requiring specific training to facilitate them, given their use for diagnostic purposes. Concerning scope of practice, counselors working in any counseling environment should consider the degree to which they can appropriately and effectively utilize assessments to investigate the connection between career development and mental health.

Practice

Concerning counseling practice, it is sometimes challenging to determine the primary aim of the therapeutic engagement. Clients and students will often come to counseling with complex concerns related to both career and mental health. The perspective of the counseling practitioner concerning their capability to address either career or mental health concerns can greatly influence how they treat integrated concerns. As a licensed clinical mental health counselor who has worked in a university career center and prepared counseling students for the field of counseling, I can attest to the differing attitudes of counselors and students concerning the importance of career and the necessary competence required to address co-occurring concerns.

The integration of career and mental health within the provision of services has been indicated. Those receiving services should have continuity of care in which support for their career and mental health concerns includes consistent messaging from a unified team of providers (Drake & Bond, 2008). The inclusion of mental health in the provision of employment support often occurs by proxy, requiring providers who work in these settings to understand the impact of mental health on career development (Gatesy-Davis et al., 2022).

Although counselors in CACREP-accredited programs are required to complete a course in career development and counseling (CACREP, 2023), instructors who teach the career course have indicated that many students display a negative attitude about having to take the course (Osborn & Dames, 2013). Furthermore, students often have misconceptions about the interrelationships between career and personal counseling. In addition, counselors-in-training without previous experience in career-focused counseling lack a framework to understand the value of career counseling and have little belief in their ability to facilitate focus on career in counseling (Lara et al., 2011). This discrepancy often manifests in the lack of self-efficacy for counseling practitioners who work in career settings to address aspects of mental health, as well as the inverse of those who work in mental health settings being uncertain of their skills in addressing career concerns (Vaingankar et al., 2021).

In my experience as a counselor educator and supervisor, novice counselors have shared their surprise at how often career-related concerns are a focus of their work with those they serve. Regardless of their initial motivation to learn about career-focused counseling, they encounter situations in which the connection between career development and mental health concerns emerges. Their competence in addressing these concerns is then examined to determine next steps in their work with clients or students.

The similarities and differences between psychotherapy, counseling, and career counseling have been discussed in the counseling literature (McIlveen, 2015). Niles and Anderson (1995) conducted an extensive review of counseling sessions in a community counseling setting, which indicated significant overlap between these areas. Career interventions are, in fact, psychological interventions, given the breadth and depth of career concerns (Niles & Harris-Bowlsbey, 2021). These perspectives make delineating career counseling versus mental health counseling difficult to determine.

For those with a clinical mental health counseling identity and engage in diagnosing, dimensions of career are integrated into this process. Challenges and impairment with occupational functioning are included in the criteria for several diagnoses (e.g., bipolar I and II, major depressive disorder, posttraumatic stress disorder) (American Psychiatric Association, 2022). The National Career Development Association Code of Ethics (2024) mentions diagnosing as an element of practice, emphasizing that "Career development professionals take special care to provide proper diagnosis and recommendations and do so only when making a diagnosis is appropriate and when properly trained" (Section E.5.a). With diagnosis, state counseling statutes and regulations often determine the ability of practitioners to engage in this practice regardless of setting. Awareness of the interconnection between these variables is essential to engage effectively in the diagnostic process.

Within school counseling, the American School Counseling Association indicates that the work of school counselors entails supporting students in their academic, career, and social/emotional development (ASCA; American School Counseling Association, n.d.). The ASCA National Model (2019) also focuses on career readiness, including career development, firmly situated in the school counselors' scope of practice. As a product of this inclusion, mental health factors relevant to academic and career considerations will emerge, requiring knowledge of these factors and an integrated response from the school counselor to address these concerns.

Regardless of the setting in which they provide services, counselors need to consider the degree to which they possess the requisite knowledge and training to address the needs of those they serve. Though the required course on career development and counseling in CACREP-accredited programs is an introduction to this topic, continued training and consideration of career development and its specific connection to aspects of mental health are needed to respond appropriately to complex career and mental health concerns. It is essential to ensure that approaches and models to address co-occurring career and mental health challenges provide relevant and responsive frameworks to holistically support the client or student.

Differentiated Service Delivery Model

When considering ways to account for career development and mental health integration within counseling services, counselors need to determine the degree and amount of support to provide. As mentioned in Chapter 5, counseling is a scarce resource, emphasizing the importance of organizing services to offer increased access to individuals based on their assessed needs (Sampson et al., 2011).

The differentiated service delivery model, focused on assessing readiness and aligning the modality of support from a brief engagement to a more protracted modality, such as individual counseling service delivery, offers a framework to increase access (Sampson & Lenz, 2023). The components of this approach involve 1) understanding the needs of the client, 2) recommending career-focused assessment and intervention to the one being served, 3) orienting the client to effectively use information to address their needs, and 4) following up to assess the client's use of the information to address their concerns. A significant increase in access to services has been found by assessing need and providing a commensurate amount of service via the differentiated service delivery model (Sampson et al., 2017). Accounting for both experiences of career and mental health within this framework enables a practitioner to determine the depth and breadth of support needed by those being served.

Though a clear delineation concerning career development and mental health may exist within the counseling training and organizational structure of counseling agencies, the likelihood of encountering individuals with co-occurring career and mental health concerns requires an informed and sophisticated framework that accounts for this relationship. Expanding one's scope of practice through experience, supervision, and training enables counselors to operate within an appropriate scope of practice reflective of the lived experience of those being served.

Referral

There are instances in which mental health concerns are so pronounced that counseling provided by practitioners who focus on mental health is required. When this emerges, a continuum of care between career-focused and mental health-focused providers is a desirable framework as this ensures the appropriate level of support is provided with an eye toward integrating career and mental health support. Mental health concerns such as depression and trauma may require protracted support, while career concerns are often time-bound and necessitate a specific action on the part of the individual being served (Hayden et al., 2023).

Acknowledging the inherent barriers between these areas of focus within counseling is essential. When working with youth with severe mental health conditions, the importance of including vocation is acknowledged along with barriers to integrated service delivery. Barriers to integrating mental health and vocational services include the lack of knowledge of the services provided within each organization and a different philosophy related to the vocational needs of transition-age youth with mental health needs (Gatesy-Davis et al., 2022). These barriers complicate the referral process as counselors cannot provide an informed referral that will appropriately address identified needs.

Collaboration Between Providers

With this in mind, siloed career and mental health services are not responsive to the nature of the concerns. An informed referral characterizes an appropriate referral structure in which a counselor is aware of the nature of available career and mental health services, along with consistent communication between career and mental health services. An analogous experience within counseling would be the use of psychiatric services in conjunction with traditional talk therapy provided by a counselor. The skills used by those involved in this collaboration between providers are applicable in this instance.

I remember one experience when considering the connection between career development and mental health. While serving as a program director at a university career center, I worked with an individual who requested a résumé critique, a common service provided by the career center. In my time with the student, it became apparent that concerns existed beyond the quality of the résumé. After some exploration, I determined that the student needed support from the counseling center. I walked the student directly there and connected her with a professional counselor. My previous work experience with the counseling center, in which we engaged in shared training and consistently communicated through various university forums, provided a context in which our collaborative support could benefit this student. This collaboration emphasized the importance of knowing what resources are available and the actual people serving as providers, all working for the benefit of the student.

There are examples of ways to effectively integrate career development and mental health within service delivery that demonstrate an integrated scope of practice. Programs recognized for providing career services to young adults offer a blueprint for effectively integrating career and mental health counseling services. Key features of these programs include detailed and written planning, working closely with families, inter-agency collaboration, and the use of normative community resources (Ellison et al., 2018). Though the study's subjects were young adults, focusing on connecting services and including invested parties, such as those associated with the individuals receiving services, offers insight into how to effectively integrate career and mental health services.

In terms of the organizational structure of counseling services, focusing on specific considerations can contribute to an effective integration of career and mental health services. Within higher education, where career and mental health services are typically separated, examining institutional policies, the administrative structure, available clinical space, record-keeping practices, available resources, professional identities of providers, counseling supervision, training, and professional liability are indicated as necessary within the integration of career and mental health support (Lenz et al., 2010). Building and sustaining counseling services that consistently organize services to account for the connection of career development and mental health is essential in responding to the integration of these domains.

Recommendations for Integration of Services and Scope of Practice

From this information, the following are recommendations on integrating career development and mental health in counseling and consideration for counseling practice. Regardless of the counseling setting, a commitment to integration informed by the wealth of research supporting the relationship between career development and mental health will enable counselors to holistically support those they serve.

First, counselors should reflect on their own personal and professional experiences with career development and mental health. Often, when I provide training on the integration of career and mental health, I ask the audience to consider five things that have helped them in their career development and five things that have hindered this process. I ask them to give additional consideration to how these elements are connected. Invariably, "family," "finances," and "opportunities" are identified as either helping or hindering career development. It is often surprising how participants make the connections between these elements, grounding their understanding of the connection between career and mental health in personal experience. Regarding professional practice, novice and experienced counselors consistently share with me times in which career and mental health intersected in the concerns of clients and students. Counselors taking the time to reflect on their own personal and professional experiences with this integration will add context to the importance of this topic within their work.

Second, ongoing professional development on career- and mental health-related concerns is essential. The ACA and the NCDA Codes of Ethics speak to operating within areas of competence related to experience, supervision, and training. Attending training that focuses on a topic not immediately within their usual menu of professional practices (e.g., mental health providers receiving career-focused professional development and vice versa with career practitioners attending mental health-focused training) offers a means for counselors to cross-pollinate their understanding of these topics. The National Career Development Association and the Center for Credentialing and Education offer certifications in career development.

Third, an extension of professional development includes accessing the professional literature on career development and mental health integration. The *Journal of Counseling & Development*, *The Career Development Quarterly*, the *Journal of Vocational Behavior*, the *Journal of Employment Counseling*, and the *British Journal of Guidance & Counselling* contain scholarly articles on the integration of career and mental health. *Counseling Today* also contains practitioner-focused articles that discuss career development and mental health elements. Staying current with relevant information on the interconnection between career and mental health is essential for providing effective and responsive counseling services.

Fourth, systematic evaluation of services in which counselors assess the impact of their work on dimensions of career development and mental health is strongly encouraged. The empirical examination of outcome research on these topics, such as that presented in this text, is extensive. While this information helps inform practice, counselors have the opportunity to evaluate the impact and quality of their efforts to address this integration. Innovative interventions can also be evaluated for their effectiveness.

Finally, consistent connection between providers with an area of focus outside that of the counselors can enhance awareness of best practices and trends in either area. Those who work in mental health environments will benefit from contact with those who work in career-focused environments and vice versa. As the career and mental health factors evolve, this engagement with practitioners working in career and mental health settings will provide insight into the dynamic nature of these experiences within the populations they serve.

The integration of counseling services and scope of practice concerning career development and mental health has several dimensions. Given the evidence of the association between these domains and the benefits of integrating these topics within counseling services, counselors should assess and treat them simultaneously. This will require an ongoing commitment on the practitioner's part to identify areas of strength and opportunities for growth in integrating these topics within counseling. Through this work, individuals receiving services will benefit from this holistic approach.

Conclusion

Integrating career development and mental health in practice requires intention and effort across various aspects of service delivery. Identifying assessment and intervention strategies that integrate them enables counselors in various settings to respond to the needs of those they serve. In instances in which a referral for either mental health or career-specific support is to the benefit of the client, continuing to look for ways to simultaneously address these concerns through collaboration between providers is essential to ensuring continuity of care is established. Ongoing professional development on emerging career and mental health needs, along with strategies to address these needs, is necessary for the effective integration of counseling services.

Pro Tips for Providers

- Reflect on your personal and professional experience with career development and mental health to determine how these domains have influenced each other.
- Consider the impact of one's professional identity and scope of practice on their willingness to engage with those they serve in aspects of career development and mental health.
- Assess one's comfort level in providing counseling services focused on integrated career and mental health concerns.
- Develop competence in counseling, addressing either domain (i.e., career or mental health) through ongoing training and professional development.
- Examine organizational structures and ethos to determine how barriers to integrated career development and mental health services create siloed services.
- Seek consultation, supervision, and support from other practitioners to determine how career development and mental health support can appropriately reflect the lived experience of those being served.
- Advocate for the integration of career development and mental health services in various counseling settings to remove barriers to holistic counseling support that appropriately reflects the lived experience of those being served.

Views from the Field

Brian Calhoun
Associate Professor of the Practice, Wake Forest University Department of Education

Career development and mental health should be incorporated into vocational university courses. At the undergraduate level, many instances necessitate the use of integrated career, mental health, and culturally responsive interventions. As college classes and assignments may cause anxiety, there is a great need to be aware of students' mental health and well-being. Through reflections and active listening during classroom interactions, one can assist and be responsive to students' needs during their career and academic journey. I have noticed that students overwhelmed with course loads require greater flexibility in scheduling and alternative ways to reflect on their learning.

"Counselors engage in assessment practices every day, and these practices affect relationships, treatment decisions, and culturally responsive counseling" (Hays, 2024). The same can be said for career counselors working in a career center or classroom. For students, contacting someone for an informational interview for the first time can often create anxiety. Career counselors must be aware and culturally sensitive when asking students to reach out to an individual they might not know very well. Prompts and conversation starters may assist in the process. It is also worth noting that electronic introductions, or starting with a person familiar to the student, may also decrease anxiety. I always try to connect students with people familiar with working with students who might not have conducted an informational interview in the past.

Additional areas of communicating vocational assessment results must also be considered. "Future trends in assessment, including ways that counselors can expect to respond to issues such as a changing cultural landscape, globalization, and technology" (Hays, 2024). When providing students with assessment results, one must be mindful to fully explain how the data may be interpreted. Providing additional resources and ways to look at career assessment can also reduce anxiety and mental fatigue. Assessments may give insight into certain directions but are not meant to provide the ultimate direction. Working with students directly and listening to what they are looking for in their future academic and career pursuits is vitally important. I am glad to have a university partner such as the WFU Center for Learning, Access, and Student Success (CLASS) office that assists with providing students with assessments and accommodations. This partnership is invaluable for students and faculty to look for greater accessibility to learning.

Direct meetings and communication with students in class provide the ultimate feedback and relationship-building necessary for culturally responsive career counseling and development. Technology should assist and not impede a student's journey to secure employment. I am a part of the technology accessibility committee on campus to keep reviewing and being aware of accessibility issues as it pertains to educational technology.

I find that conversations with peers and students in the classroom have the potential to give classroom participants the greatest opportunity to achieve a greater perspective on what they want to achieve post-college. In the classes I teach, I may have non-traditional students who have not been in the classroom for some time. Additional time and support need to be provided in these instances. As educational technology and learning platforms continue to evolve, we need to be aware of these changes and communicate with our students on how to best interact with educational technology.

As career counselors, we continue to make assessments daily. It is our responsibility to understand the goals of our clients and students. By observing non-verbal cues and listening, we can assist our clients. Communication is at the heart of this process.

7

Ethical Dimensions of Career and Mental Health Support

When providing integrated career and mental health services, several questions emerge. What ethical concerns arise when providing career and mental health services? How do I operate ethically when equally focusing on career and mental health in my work? What resources are available to me to resolve ethical concerns and dilemmas? Chapter 6 touches on some of these elements within the discussion of scope of practice. Additional ethical dimensions within integrated career and mental health services include confidentiality, client safety, personal values and beliefs, and ethical principles such as beneficence, nonmaleficence, and veracity. Counselors are often faced with complex concerns spanning across the human experience, requiring thoughtful consideration of the complexity of career and mental health concerns. Accordingly, a consideration of ethics within practice is needed.

Integrating career and mental health in counseling is not simply a useful consideration but, in some ways, an ethical mandate due to the established connection between these domains and the impact of integrated support. The separation of these topic areas within counseling is contrary to the evidence of the potential benefit of career counseling on aspects of mental health (Arifoulline et al., 2024) and counterintuitive to the human experience in these areas.

Various codes of ethics, such as those of the American Counseling Association and the National Career Development Association, provide guidance on addressing co-occurring career and mental health concerns in practice. Other codes of ethics offer insight into the ethical provision of career and mental health support. In addition, the CACREP accreditation standards (CACREP, 2023) concerning the career counseling specialization provide insight into what specifically should be taught to counselors being trained in the specific domain of career development support.

Career Counseling's Connection to Mental Health Support

In training aspiring counselors who focus on career development, the CACREP standards indicate the importance of focusing on relevant mental health factors. Factors that affect client attitudes towards work and career decision-making (CACREP, 2023, Standard 5.B.1); the unique characteristics of career exploration, employment expectations, and socioeconomic issues of diverse clients (Standard 5.B.2); the implications of gender roles on education, family, and leisure (Standard 5.B.3); and the impact of globalization on careers and the workplace (Standard 5.B.4) included within the career counseling specialization standards speak to the importance of mental health as it relates to career and the need for those focused on career to be versed in these elements.

These standards, in combination with the previously mentioned standards in the foundational counseling curriculum, further emphasize the acknowledgment of the connection between career and mental health. Ethical practice requires a cohesive framework in which these aspects of people's experience are appropriately addressed within counseling services.

Ethical Principles and Integrated Support

Operating within ethical principles indicated in the American Counseling Association (2014) and the National Career Development Association (2024a) Codes of Ethics is both essential to ethical practice and informative of the ethical dimensions of career and mental health support.

Autonomy

Autonomy speaks to fostering an individual's ability to control one's life (ACA, 2014) and is directly relevant to integrated support. When faced with challenges of career, education, and work, mental health factors can directly threaten an individual's ability to make decisions effectively and engage in experiences that enhance control and volition. As career and work can significantly impact volition, a counselor's ability to navigate both aspects within counseling can enhance agency within career development and mental health (Hayden et al., 2021).

Nonmaleficence

The principle of *nonmaleficence*—the "do no harm" axiom—is the avoidance of actions that cause harm (ACA, 2014). Nonmaleficence is also connected to the integration of career and mental health services, given the impact of struggles in either area on the other. There are instances when counselors must lean into mental health or career concerns as well as opt out of addressing particular concerns via collaboration with other providers or a potential referral, depending on the nature of the issue. As discussed in Chapter 6, scope of practice offers important considerations concerning competence to address either issue within counseling practice. Being unwilling to comprehensively address both career and mental health concerns could be considered nonmaleficence in counseling practice.

Beneficence

In addition to "do no harm," counselors are mandated to engage in practices that work for the good of individuals and society. This is very relevant to the provision of integrated support. Counselors with the capacity to address both career development and mental health concerns can minimize hardships for those receiving services by increasing access to services and eliminating the inclusion of additional providers that may not be accessible. This is evidenced by the relatively low percentage of those who accept referrals to mental health counselors, especially for certain populations (Moothedan et al., 2024).

Improvements in career development and mental health counseling benefit broader society and those within it, requiring counselors to consider ways to integrate these two areas. Utilizing integrated career assessments (Chapter 3) and frameworks (Chapter 4) aligns with beneficence as it accounts for the depth of the concern and enhances the likelihood of positive outcomes in both domains.

Veracity

The principle of *veracity*, in which the counselor is truthful with clients receiving services, is imperative in navigating career and mental health concerns (ACA, 2014). This certainly pertains to career-focused counselors when addressing mental health concerns. There are licensed counselors who operate within career services who have to determine their ability to address mental health concerns within their context (NCDA, 2024a). This also applies to mental health-focused providers' ability to navigate aspects of career development. Sharing the degree of competence and experience the counselor possesses in addressing co-occurring issues is essential to enabling those receiving services to determine the degree to which these topics will be covered within counseling.

Client Safety

While the benefits of integrated support have been previously mentioned, there are risks to client safety. I have had several experiences in which career and mental health rose to the level of potential harm to the client. There have been instances in which career concerns quickly evolved into mental health crisis work. When engaging a client with relation to career concerns, counselors should be aware of the degree of severity of the client's mental health concerns—career concerns are also high stakes as one's future, livelihood, and access to income and resources are impacted by career uncertainty that can, in turn, impacts mental health.

The increase in the use of technology, such as distance counseling within integrated services, presents unique considerations for counselors. When exploring mental health issues solely or in conjunction with career, client crises may emerge. Whether providing career or mental health support, a clear plan for addressing mental health crises is essential for ensuring client safety.

Confidentiality

Confidentiality manifests in unique ways when considering the provision of integrated care. The ACA and NCDA Codes of Ethics discuss confidentiality, informed consent, and privacy. In practice, there are instances within career services where confidentiality, informed consent, and privacy depend on the setting and the professional identity of the provider. Nearly 50% of the National Career Development Association members do not have a degree in counseling (NCDA, 2024b)—therefore, considerations of informed consent and confidentiality are not universally understood in providing career services. Drop-in consultations, workshops, and career-focused events often deliver career-focused services, which creates a unique context for implementing career and mental health services integration.

Exploration of both career and mental health concerns may often broach deeply personal topics. There is the potential likelihood that an increased focus on mental health within career-focused services will heighten the consideration of confidentiality and privacy. When considering how to appropriately address these topics, being versed in facilitating these discussions and determining effective strategies for creating an environment conducive to exploring these topics is essential.

Training

Additional training may be needed to engage in ethical practice with regard to career and mental health competence in either area. Attending professional development events that examine these concepts can bolster a counselor's ability to administer integrated interventions. In addition, the National Career Development Association has several credentials designed to enable providers across disciplines to learn more about effective strategies for addressing career development concerns.

Several credentials indicate competence in a counselor's ability to navigate career development. These credentials require documented training in aspects of career development, including career theory, interventions, and other elements (NCDA, n.d.). The Certified Master of Career Services (CMCS) and Certified Career Counselor (CCC) are NCDA credentials that counselors can use to expand their understanding of the depth of career concerns and strategies for providing effective support. The Center for Credentialing and Education also has a career-focused certification, the Global Career Development Facilitator (GCDF), designed to support counselors in addressing career development concerns (Center for Credentialing & Education, n.d.).

Supervision

Any engagement in practice outside of one's competence requires support, such as supervision while venturing into new areas of focus within counseling (ACA, 2014; NCDA, 2024a). Supervision with an eye toward integration can significantly enhance the supervisee's competence in addressing co-occurring concerns. Lenz et al. (2010) mentioned the use of supervision when integrating career and mental health services, acknowledging the ethical and legal considerations of credentialing and licensure of the supervisor and the professional liability associated with this process. Referencing relevant licensure regulations and statutes, along with ethical codes concerning the supervision of counseling practice, offers a means of determining appropriate practice.

Attention has been given to how supervision can support counselors in developing competence in integrated interventions. Competence development in the assessment process, especially when dealing with career and mental health concerns, is imperative to ethical practice (Hayden & Kronholz, 2015). Hayden (2019) applied the Discrimination Model of Clinical Supervision (Bernard & Goodyear, 1979, 1997) to career-focused counseling as it incorporates the roles of *counselor, consultant,* and *teacher* with a focus on the skills of *conceptualization, intervention,* and *personalization* (adapting one's personal style to counseling while being aware of one's personal issues). This approach lends itself well to supporting counselors' ability to attend to complex concerns as it captures the connection between these domains. A supervisor operating from this perspective analyzes the different elements of counseling practice, adapting the role and focus of supervision to the needs of the counseling supervisor.

Accountability

Many critical considerations have arisen with the ever-increasing context of accountability in counseling (American School Counseling Association, 2019; Balkin & Kleist, 2022). The NCDA Code of Ethics (2024) references "evidence-informed practice" as an essential component of the ethical provision of counseling services. With this in mind, the gathering of evidence related to the effectiveness of integrated interventions benefits those being served, with data provided by counselors tracking the impact of integrated interventions on dimensions of career and mental health.

Several evaluation methods can be employed to engage ethically in providing counseling that addresses co-occurring career and mental health concerns. More feasible methods for practitioners, such as the single-subject research design and focus groups, may offer a means by which counselors can continually monitor their ability to attend to interconnected concerns. Beyond the perspective of evaluation for the sake of the individual counselor, additional attention can be given to the impact of the work on those invested in the well-being of individuals. The Accountability Bridge Model (Figure 7.11) demonstrates the unique context in which various programs are enacted and the need to develop counseling programs that are both dynamic and responsive to the needs of those impacted by outcomes (Astramovich & Coker, 2007).

Figure 7.1
The Accountability Bridge Model

Accountability Bridge Counseling Program Evaluation Model

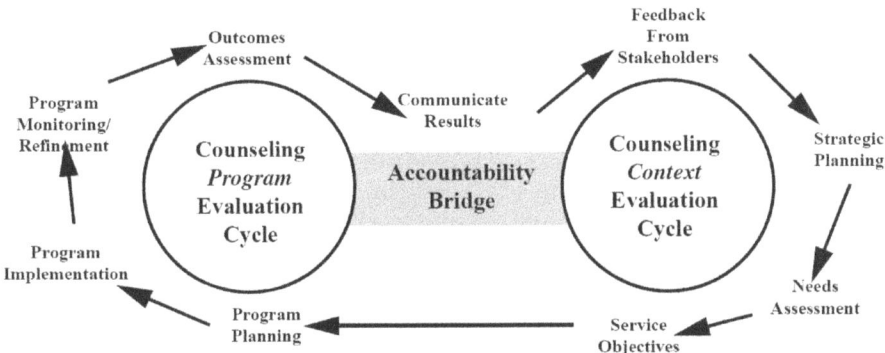

Note. Astramovich, R. L., & Coker, K. (2007). The Accountability Bridge Model: A program evaluation tool for counselors. *Journal of Counseling & Development, 85*(2), 162–172. Used with permission.

Within this framework, the Counseling Program Evaluation Cycle and the Counseling Context Evaluation Cycle interact with each other such that the counseling practitioner and those invested in outcomes are continually involved in the development and evaluation of the program. Evaluating outcomes associated with integrated career and mental health counseling is ethically necessary when considering the broader contextual career and educational forces (e.g., educational attainment, economic development, shifting demographic and occupational trends) that impact individuals and communities.

Beliefs and Values Related to Career and Work

An interesting dimension of career and mental health is the degree to which one's values and beliefs related to these domains influence both the counselor and the client. One example comes to mind: I was working with a student considering dropping out of the university. Because I believe strongly that education is one of the most important things in a person's life, I was surprised at how this belief emerged in my engagement with the client. Counselors who utilize integrated career and mental health interventions must be aware of their values and beliefs to ensure they are not violating the autonomy and volition of individuals receiving support (ACA, 2014; NCDA, 2024a). In addition, personal beliefs concerning career and work can both enhance and hinder progress toward counseling goals. Expectations and beliefs around career and work are worth assessing when addressing co-occurring concerns, a comprehensive approach essential to ethical practice.

Conclusion

When venturing into career and mental health, several ethical considerations emerge concerning the degree to which counselors are trained to address career and mental health concerns. Continually assessing one's competence and engaging in professional development that accounts for deficiencies is essential to ethical practice. Both the American Counseling Association and the National Career Development Association Codes of Ethics address critical practice components in need of attention on the part of the practitioner, as well as credentialing, training, and other means of supplementing one's ability to address interconnected career and mental health concerns (ACA, 2014; NCDA, 2024a). Utilizing resources such as supervision, program evaluation, and reflection is instrumental in the development of integrated interventions and best serves those experiencing difficulty with complex issues of career and mental health.

Pro Tips for Providers

- Reference relevant codes of ethics, such as those from the American Counseling Association a nd the National Career Development Association, to identify ethical considerations pertinent to their work.
- Evaluate the degree to which ethical principles of autonomy, beneficence, nonmaleficence, veracity, and client safety manifest in the provision of integrated career and mental health support.
- Access professional development opportunities that supplement growth and development in counseling

practice, either in the areas of career or mental health, to develop competence in addressing these topics.
- Engage in counseling supervision when appropriate to further enhance one's capability to support those experiencing co-occurring career and mental health concerns.
- Assess counseling outcomes in career and mental health factors to ensure those being served receive effective integrated counseling services.
- Reflect on personal beliefs and values regarding career and work and determine how these may impact their engagement with clients experiencing career concerns.

Views from the Field

Helen Morgan MA, NCC
Wake Forest University

One of my favorite parts about being a university career coach is that career touches everything: our values, our self-esteem and self-worth, our financial stability, our stress and anxiety levels, and often, our overall happiness and sense of purpose. When one or more of these areas is out of balance, our mental health is inevitably impacted. While the majority of my time is spent strategizing with students about career exploration, resume writing, networking, interview preparation, and job or internship searches, mental health concerns frequently arise during these action-oriented processes—particularly anxiety and self-esteem issues. With Gen-Z being a highly anxious demographic, mental health challenges are no stranger to my office, particularly at an elite and academically rigorous institution. Students consistently report feeling "behind" their peers, facing parental pressure, and worrying they'll never find a meaningful career while frequently discounting their strong experiences. In short, they often feel like they aren't enough in an ever-connected world of LinkedIn announcements and social media.

Regarding the intersection of career and mental health in a university career center, the ethical principles and techniques used for counseling remain largely consistent with those used in a traditional mental health setting (i.e., private practice, university counseling center, community mental health center, etc.). Like a counselor working in private practice, I abide by the overarching ethical principles outlined by the American Counseling Association (ACA), including autonomy, nonmaleficence, beneficence, justice, fidelity, and veracity. I frequently use theoretical orientations such as person-centered therapy and cognitive behavioral therapy.

However, my professional setting and role as a university career *coach* differ critically from that of a mental health *counselor*, particularly regarding confidentiality. Unlike counselors in mental health settings who engage in career counseling, I am *not* considered a confidential resource or required to hold an active counseling license. While I make every effort to respect and protect a student's privacy, because I am not considered a confidential resource, I am mandated to report or escalate certain incidents, particularly those related to Title IX and active suicidal ideation, whereas my colleagues in the University Counseling Center do not. In addition, part of my role is teaching career education courses, leading to a dual relationship with clients that wouldn't be ethical if I were only a mental health counselor. Similarly, while a mental health counselor cannot initiate a greeting if they were to see a client in public, I am free to do so, which often strengthens the therapeutic relationship. There have even been cases where, with their consent, it may be appropriate to connect two students I work with for networking purposes. This distinction partly stems from the perception of career counseling as more of an academic resource with fewer associated stigmas.

While some may find it surprising that mental health topics surface during career coaching sessions or courses, the trust built within the therapeutic relationships has led me to have discussions centered on mental health, ranging from relationship breakups to anxiety, panic attacks, and depression, to supporting survivors navigate the aftermath of sexual assault. While I use my counseling skills to help my students through these challenges, it is also my ethical responsibility to refer them to a dedicated mental health provider when the issue strays too far from career and requires more comprehensive support. In fact, it would be considered unethical to see a student in the career center strictly for mental health counseling, as it would be considered out of the scope of practice for the setting, even if the practitioner had an active counseling license.

With a dual role as a career education professor, career counseling course assignments can also reveal mental health challenges. For example, a student in my course submitted a reflection paper for their final exam that discussed committing suicide and harming others. In addition to a direct threat to harm themselves and others, the student had previously exhibited behaviors and shared concerns in individual appointments that led me to refer them to the counseling center for additional support. As a mandated reporter, I was required to report this scenario, particularly because it was documented in writing. While our counseling center practitioners cannot directly reach out to a student, my university has a CARE Team (Campus Assessment, Response, and Evaluation), which *can* contact an individual of concern to provide confidential services and resources. Just as in mental health counseling, documentation of observations in individual appointments, email communications, and assignments remains critical from an ethical standpoint.

Regardless of licensure, it's crucial for university career coaches to communicate the limits of confidentiality clearly and make appropriate referrals. When faced with ethical dilemmas, consulting with colleagues and supervisors is key. The intersection of career and mental health in a university setting can be complex and requires a nuanced understanding of both ethical principles as well as campus standards and dynamics. As career coaches, we are uniquely positioned to provide both career education along with guidance and support for related mental health challenges. By collaborating and triaging with mental health professionals and other campus resources, we can ensure students receive the holistic support they need while maintaining our scope of practice.

8

Case Studies

The following case studies provide insight into the application of presented information related to counseling research, theory, and practice reg arding the connection between career development and mental health. Though not comprehensive, these case studies will be similarly structured by including a description of the client/group being served, relevant characteristics of the case such as the presenting concern for the reader to develop a detailed case conceptualization, delivered interventions, and considerations for broader application. As this text is designed to help counseling practitioners develop their understanding of the connection between career development and mental health and apply this specifically to counseling practice, this section is structured with this in mind.

The case studies are focused on various counseling environments. Within these environments, professional counselors encounter a wide range of concerns on the part of those they serve. The characteristics of each case are provided to inform the response to the scenario, with prescribed questions to structure the processing of each case study. The information that has been shared is the primary resource for informing the consideration of each case study.

Relevant issues such as career readiness, life transitions, trauma-informed care, and appropriate interventions will be embedded within the case studies. The reader is asked to conceptualize and respond to each scenario with an eye toward an integrated career development and mental health approach. The previous discussion of theories, assessments, contextual and internal factors, and integrated interventions is an essential resource in shaping the response of a counselor.

The inclusion of specific environments and topics does not minimize the importance of various topics not discussed in the case studies. The application of this information is hopefully general enough to apply to other scenarios that emerge in a professional counselor's work. Each of the following case studies will have guiding questions for examination, offering a framework to process the case's specific details. Though some cases may seem more relevant than others, analyzing all of the case studies will enhance the reader's application of this information within counseling practice.

Career and Mental Health in K-12 Schools

Jeremiah is a 17-year-old student who identifies as a Black male. The school he attends is in a middle-class area of town known for its success in sports and the arts. His physics teacher advises the extracurricular physics club that Jeremiah is a member of, and the teacher has thus recognized Jeremiah's high capability in the subject matter both in the classroom and the club. Jeremiah has expressed uncertainty about his post-secondary career plans. His teacher, aware of Jeremiah's concerns, has referred him to his school counselor, Jennifer.

Eager for clarity on next steps after graduation, Jeremiah meets with Jennifer. He shared that physics comes easily to him but doesn't know how to find an option that is both financially doable and maintains his interest. Jeremiah described his current social connections with other students as somewhat limited, as his family moved to the area a little over a year ago due to a parental job relocation. He described enjoying other subjects as well, especially art. Although strongly interested in art, he doesn't believe it will be a viable pathway for his career and work. Jeremiah's family is supportive and emphasizes the importance of academic success.

Both parents completed advanced degrees in their respective fields and strongly value higher education. Jeremiah is the middle child of three, with an older brother attending college and a younger sister in 9th grade at the same school. He describes his relationship with his siblings as "strong," and he greatly admires his older brother and his perceived success both academically and socially. He speaks of receiving both implicit and explicit messages from his parents and close relatives about their desire for him to be successful, like his older brother.

Jeremiah expresses his interest in exploring careers in physics but is unaware of others "who look like me" working in those jobs. During the same session with Jennifer, he also reports experiencing instances of bullying, discrimination, and the use of racial pejoratives by fellow students at school, particularly in the after-school extracurricular activities he participates in twice a week.

Jennifer has previously met with Jeremiah regarding ongoing concerns about the student bullying, but also, alarmingly, bullying by a school staff member who works in the after-school program. Jeremiah had indicated that the issue was "no big deal" and that he just wanted to "let it go" without involving other students. Jennifer has experience providing career support to students individually and in classroom guidance.

How would you respond as a counselor to this scenario? In responding, it is encouraged to continually determine how the connection between career development and mental health manifests. For this scenario, it is critical to determine the degree to which discrimination and racism are impacting Jeremiah. This contextual consideration will have implications for both the client and the counselor.

Guiding Questions for Jeremiah's Case

1. What are Jeremiah's primary concerns? List them in order of importance, based on the priority of attention within the counseling engagement.
2. What are the relevant career and mental health factors impacting Jeremiah's experience?
3. What additional information would be helpful to know to inform your response to the case study?
4. What career theories seem appropriate for addressing the co-occurring career development and mental health factors?
5. How should Jennifer effectively assess the degree of relevant career and mental health factors impacting the client's experience? Indicate ways in which Jennifer would process the assessment results with Jeremiah.
6. To what degree does Jennifer's counseling environment impact the counselor's work addressing career and mental health factors?
7. What counseling framework(s) discussed in Chapter 2 seem best suited to address the experience of the subject of the case study? Provide a justification for your response.

8. In Jeremiah's case, what integrated interventions address the connection between career development and mental health?
9. What other factors in Jeremiah's case might be worth consideration?

Career and Mental Health in Community Agencies

Sophia identifies as a biracial (Latina/White) 46-year-old female. She is married and a mother of two school-aged children. She has come to the family services office in her community due to the low-cost counseling services for help with self-reported "depression." Upon the completion of her initial intake form, she was referred to José, a counselor who works at the community agency and specializes in addressing depression.

Sophia tells José she works as a receptionist at a primary care physician's office. She has worked there for two years and indicated it is not "the best place to work" because it is a stressful environment in which the practice's physicians are very demanding of the staff in terms of work attendance and the timely completion of tasks. Sophia indicates that there have been instances when she has missed work due to familial issues and received negative feedback about consistent attendance in her annual evaluations. She took the job due to her family's financial needs after moving to the area because of her husband's work starting up retail stores for a large clothing company. They have moved several times since they have been married due to her husband's job requirements.

Sophia has earned a bachelor's degree in English literature and reports being an "avid reader." She also likes to write poetry but has not had much time to do this of late due to familial and work commitments. She reports growing up in a household that was not supportive of her in general, specifically about her decision to pursue English literature as a major in college, as you can't "support yourself with that type of degree." She persisted in pursuing the degree, nonetheless, due to her love of the subject matter and her desire to be somewhat defiant of her parents.

Sophia reports a close relationship with her husband and children, though the husband is not a "big talker." She has not communicated her frustration with her current work to him, as he was "really excited" about the family's relocation. Also, with the financial resources Sophia receives from her job, they can afford to send their children to a prestigious private school in their community.

Guiding Questions for Sophia's Case

1. What are Sophia's primary concerns? List them in order of importance, based on the priority of attention within the counseling engagement.
2. What are the relevant career and mental health factors impacting Sophia's experience?
3. What additional information would be helpful to know to inform your response to the case study?
4. What career theories seem appropriate for addressing the co-occurring career development and mental health factors?
5. How should José effectively assess the degree of relevant career and mental health factors impacting the client's experience? Indicate ways in which José would process the assessment results with Sophia.
6. To what degree does José's counseling environment impact the counselor's work addressing career and mental health factors?
7. What counseling framework(s) discussed in Chapter 2 seem best suited to address the experience of the subject of the case study? Provide a justification for your response.
8. In Sophia's case, what integrated interventions address the connection between career development and mental health?
9. What other factors in Sophia's case might be worth consideration?

Career and Mental Health in Private Practice

Trevor is a Black counselor who identifies as male and works in a private practice in a rural area in the southeastern United States. He has been in private practice for several years, focusing on a wide range of mental health concerns such as anxiety, depression, and trauma. Recognizing the impact of trauma on those he serves, he sought certification in Eye Movement Desensitization and Reprocessing (EMDR). Trevor operates from an existential therapy approach (i.e., a focus on free will, self-determination, and search for meaning) as he sees critical concerns people face tied to core elements of their viewpoints of themselves, others, and the world. He has been reasonably successful in his practice, which consists of a consistent pool of clients and referrals from various sources. He is considered a well-respected helper in the community.

A recent development emerged in the community that has affected those who live there. The local manufacturing plant, which employed a significant number of community members, has relocated to another location. Though the company provided temporary financial support for employees affected by the transition, the closing has negatively impacted employment prospects as the town relied on the facility to supply a significant proportion of the high-wage jobs in the community. This has had a significantly adverse impact on the community regarding the quality of life of those within it.

Since the closing was announced and the subsequent loss of jobs, Trevor has observed an increase in mental health concerns, such as anxiety, depression, and stress in the community. While the need for services has been consistent over time, he has experienced a spike in inquiries for counseling services. In addition, his current clients speak more about their uncertainty about work and its impact on them. Carmen, one of Trevor's newer clients, came to him for counseling due to difficulties in her marriage. She and her husband have been married for quite some time, and Carmen reported reasonable relational satisfaction until recently. She was recently notified that her position in the company would be moved to a new location, a significant distance from their current community. Carmen has three young children and is the primary income earner in the family. Their family is closely connected with relatives who live in the area. One of their children also has a disability that requires specific services that are provided by their local school system at no additional cost.

Carmen indicates stress associated with her uncertain work situation and its impact on her family. Carmen's husband has become frustrated with her as she has not decided whether to accept the position in the new location. He favors the move, but Carmen does not want to relocate right now. She has three weeks from this point in time to inform the company of her decision. In addition, her insurance will change, meaning she will need to pay out of pocket for Trevor's services as he will become an out-of-network provider.

Guiding Questions for Carmen's Case

1. What are the primary concerns for Carmen? List them in order of importance, based on the priority of attention within the counseling engagement.
2. What are the relevant career and mental health factors impacting Carmen's experience?
3. What additional information would be helpful to know to inform your response to the case study?

4. What career theories seem appropriate for addressing the co-occurring career development and mental health factors?
5. How should Trevor effectively assess the degree of relevant career and mental health factors impacting the client's experience? Indicate ways in which Trevor would process the assessment results with Carmen.
6. To what degree does Trevor's counseling environment impact the counselor's work addressing career and mental health factors?
7. What counseling framework(s) discussed in Chapter 2 seem best suited to address the experience of the subject of the case study? Provide a justification for your response.
8. In Carmen's case, what integrated interventions address the connection between career development and mental health?
9. What other factors in Carmen's case might be worth consideration?

Career and Mental Health in Governmental Agency Counseling

Robert is a White clinical mental health counselor who identifies as male. He works in the Personalized Career Planning and Guidance program in the Veterans Administration, a governmental agency that supports military veterans. Since his time in graduate school pursuing a counseling degree, his main interest has been serving veterans transitioning from the military to civilian life. Though Robert did not serve in the military, he became interested in serving this population because of his experience growing up in a military family.

Robert encounters Stephanie, a female-identifying military veteran who served in the U.S. Navy for several years. She has sought career services as she has struggled with securing meaningful employment since her separation from the military five years ago. She has worked in several technology support jobs, aligning with her role in the Navy as an information systems technician. She has found these jobs to be financially lucrative but unfulfilling.

In Robert's discussions with Stephanie, she shared that during her time in the military, she was a victim of sexual assault on several occasions. This emerged from their consideration of various occupational options and her indication of not wanting to work in predominantly male fields. She did not report the assaults to her superiors during her time in the military because she feared the impact this would have on her relations with others in the military and her potential opportunities for advancement.

Though not related to Stephanie's presenting concern, their exploration has led to Stephanie reporting symptoms of posttraumatic stress disorder, such as intrusive thoughts, persistent avoidance of positions that involve completing projects with coworkers, and becoming extremely angry when encountering obstacles to completing tasks in her job.

Stephanie reported wanting to focus on her career concern as she is working to keep her mental health concern "under wraps" for now. Though he works in career-focused services, Robert is a licensed clinical mental health counselor and is concerned about Stephanie's overall well-being.

Guiding Questions for Stephanie's Case

1. What are the primary concerns for Stephanie? List them in order of importance, based on the priority of attention within the counseling engagement.
2. What are the relevant career and mental health factors impacting Stephanie's experience?
3. What additional information would be helpful to know to inform your response to the case study?
4. What career theories seem appropriate for addressing the co-occurring career development and mental health factors?
5. How should Robert effectively assess the degree of relevant career and mental health factors impacting the client's experience? Indicate ways in which Robert would process the assessment results with Stephanie.
6. To what degree does Robert's counseling environment impact the counselor's work addressing career and mental health factors?
7. What counseling framework(s) discussed in Chapter 2 seem best suited to address the experience of the subject of the case study? Provide a justification for your response.
8. In Stephanie's case, what integrated interventions address the connection between career development and mental health?
9. What other factors in Stephanie's case might be worth consideration?

9

Future Directions of Integrated Career and Mental Health Counseling

Given the complexity of the human experience, counseling services must mirror the connection between career development and mental health. Past and current experience within counseling has involved a vacillation between a focus on integrating career development and mental health and separating these elements (Redekopp & Huston, 2019).

In this "ever-changin' world in which we're livin'" (McCartney, P., McCartney, L., 1973), counselors are consistently asked to respond to both anticipated and unanticipated realities. An illustrative example is the COVID-19 pandemic, which significantly impacted the entire globe. At the time, counselors tasked with supporting clients did so in an environment that was uniformly demonstrative of the uncertainty that pervades human existence. "The world in which we're livin'," as Paul McCartney notes, is, in fact, "ever-changin'"—a reminder that change itself is constant.

Regarding the connection between career development and mental health, shifts in the marketplace create a context in which counseling resides. These shifts include emerging careers and modes of work and our expanded understanding of the impact of systems and experiences that both contribute to and deter people from realizing a fulfilling and meaningful existence. Being responsive to these conditions while utilizing evidence-based practices and established frameworks can be challenging.

The unpredictability of the world makes prognosticating about the future of counseling services as it pertains to the integration of career development and mental health potentially an exercise in futility. Who could have foreseen the pandemic as a world-changing event that would alter the trajectory of people and the counseling profession? That being said, there are predictable elements related to career and mental health that sustain relevance through the shifting sands of the world. This chapter will specifically focus on the future integration of these topics within counseling services. As this has not been discussed extensively, there is little to build on regarding previous viewpoints. With this in mind, a fair amount of what is offered here is derived from my observations of developments in practice and research.

Practice Considerations

There are several considerations concerning the future direction of career and mental health integration within counseling services. The evolving landscape of an individual's experience in career and mental health coincides with the evolving nature of counseling services. Counselors are tasked with being aware of the needs of their clients while also adapting to the shifting conditions of service delivery. Integrating career development and mental health mirrors trends in the counseling profession while also adding specific considerations.

Complex Needs and Individualized Services

The increase in mental health concerns and growing awareness of its connection to career and work will limit the ability of practitioners and mental health systems to focus solely on one domain. The mental health needs of the population are significant: recent research indicates that 21% of adults have reported experiencing a mental health concern, 16% of youth reported a major depressive episode in the past year, 4.8% of adults reported serious thoughts of suicide, and 11% of adults who identify as two or more racial groups reported serious thoughts of suicide (Reinert et al., 2022). This is coupled with 55.5% of adults with mental health concerns and, more specifically, 93.5% of adults with substance use issues not receiving treatment (Reinert et al.). Concerning career, 33.1% of cisgender men, 35.7% of women, and

43.4 transgender/non-conforming college students report problems or challenges with career in the last year (American College Health Association, 2023). In addition, the top issue (49%) reported for military families is military spouse employment (Blue Star Families, 2024). The significant need for career and mental health support reported within various populations necessitates an integrated approach responsive to the need. In addition, an increased awareness of the impact of trauma on mental and physical health has been identified as a prominent trend in the future of counseling (Rollins, 2021). Developing career and mental health delivery systems in which every contact with someone seeking care is viewed through the lens of integration is essential to effective and responsive support.

A shift from manualized to individualized modalities of practice has been indicated in the literature on the future of counseling services. A meta-analysis of standardized versus personalized interventions indicated a small but significant benefit to mental health outcomes for those receiving individual services (Nye et al., 2023). This aligns with previously mentioned concepts of readiness (e.g., Sampson et al., 2023 in Chapter 4) within integrated frameworks and the importance of not utilizing a one-size-fits-all approach in counseling.

An interesting consideration is the focus on processes of change in future counseling work (Hayes, 2023). Counseling approaches such as motivational interviewing (Miller & Rollnick, 2023) and cognitive information processing (CIP; Sampson et al., 2023) have focused on process elements to address concerns. In the future of integrated services, focusing on the individual's capability and process for navigating interrelated concerns is essential. This learning dimension focuses on the counselor and the individual collaboratively developing strategies to address career and mental health concerns. Addressing current career and mental health concerns is essential while also applying the lessons learned to similar future challenges—a critical consideration for the future of integrated career and mental health support.

Technology

Telehealth, though a longstanding methodology used in counseling services, saw a significant increase in usage due to the COVID-19 pandemic. Before the pandemic, counseling providers who made telehealth modality claims were 1% in February 2020. This increased to about 20% in March of 2020 and 53–59% in April of the same year, with 40% still using this modality at the end of 2021 (Mulvaney-Day et al., 2022). In addition, online career-focused counseling has been found to enhance career decision-making with dimensions of mental health (i.e., hardiness and psychological capital), contributing to positive outcomes (Pordelan & Hosseinian, 2021). Telehealth and distance counseling, both career- and mental health-focused, will continue to be frequently utilized. With this in mind, it raises important questions about the ability of counselors to identify and address the intersection of these concerns within people's experiences.

Given the aforementioned increase in career and mental health concerns and the limitations in resources, micro-interventions are one way in which counselors are attempting to respond to this increased need. Nudges in which those receiving services are encouraged to partake in an activity are one method of providing additional support (Hayes, 2023). These nudges and other interventions are often delivered through app-based support. The significant increase in the proliferation of handheld devices is indicated by the 96% of those between the ages of 18 and 29 who own smartphones (Pew Research Center, 2024). Several university counseling and well-being centers have developed apps that provide these nudges and other activities to offer microsupport to students (Mowreader, 2023). While there are online platforms that assist with specific job search tasks and strategies, such as LinkedIn and Glassdoor, there are few resources related to supporting career decision-making and problem-solving. Coupled with the consideration of the importance of integrating career development and mental health, we see a space in the future for integrating support for the development of online applications.

While technology is increasingly intersecting with career and mental health services, there needs to be some consideration of its benefits and challenges for counseling. The benefits include the extended reach of services, constant access, immediate response, and the generation of information gathering. Challenges include limited access to the internet, digital illiteracy, the quality of information, confidentiality, and addressing a client's urgent needs (Zainudin et al., 2020). Future efforts to integrate career and mental health support will emphasize the advantages of technology and telehealth while addressing limitations such as resource access and providers' ability to deliver high-quality information, resources, and services. A systematic approach to implementing technology and an ongoing evaluation of its benefits are essential for providing effective integrated services.

Artificial intelligence (AI) is rapidly transforming the societal landscape, particularly in counseling, career, and mental health. The development of AI has grown exponentially and is expected to play an increasingly significant role in society (Hanna, 2024). Considerable attention has been given to AI's impact on mental health care (e.g., Abrams, 2023; American Counseling Association, n.d.). While much of the focus is on AI's effects, it is critical to consider how these broader trends in counseling services intersect with efforts to integrate career and mental health support.

The impact of AI is twofold: it affects individuals navigating a rapidly changing landscape where AI reshapes tasks and jobs, often causing stress and uncertainty—even for counselors. Additionally, AI significantly influences the provision of counseling services. As this text is being written, advances in the capabilities of AI in performing tasks make predictions of how career, work, and counseling services will change very difficult to determine. When working with clients, it is becoming vital to assess how much AI and other technology are specifically affecting their work and overall well-being. Considering the integration of career and mental health within the context of these developments will enable counselors to respond accordingly to the impact of these elements on those they serve.

Relevant Trends

Counselors must also consider the context of several societal trends within the marketplace that impact career and mental health. The global economy expands this context to broader forces and trends. This presents both benefits and challenges to individuals concerning career development and mental health (Hayden et al., 2023). Interestingly, I have been fortunate to engage with counselors in other countries (e.g., Australia, China, Germany, Lebanon, and Singapore), and they have indicated an increase in attention to mental health in general and specifically within the workplace.

Alternative methods of work are another trend that impacts individuals. As with most innovations in career and work, multiple facets benefit and hinder career development and mental health. Being able to work remotely, flexible scheduling, job-sharing, and other trends have provided multiple modalities of work (Reardon et al., 2023). The benefits of flexibility exist simultaneously with the increased intrusion into spaces outside the workplace, such as the home. In addition, the advent of the "gig economy," in which people operate as freelance workers, has experienced significant growth in the last decade (Delouya, 2023). As with other developments in the world of work, the advantages come with challenges. In the United States, these types of jobs offer a buffer for those experiencing unemployment and provide flexibility in work schedules but often lack benefits like health insurance, reflecting the link between employment and access to this essential resource. Acknowledging and assessing the multiple facets of alternative employment impact is an important consideration for the future of integrated career and mental health services.

These trends generally contribute to a shifting career and work landscape, impacting mental health dimensions. As we move forward, the effects of these trends will continue to evolve, creating opportunities and challenges for both counselors and those receiving services. Staying abreast of relevant trends will enable counselors focused on integrating career and mental health to respond effectively to the needs of those they serve.

The diversification of society due to newly arrived immigrants and population shifts requires counselors to consider the specific needs of various populations. Paying attention to the unique career and mental health needs of these populations, such as those who are traditionally marginalized (see Chapter 4), is imperative to the provision of holistic support.

Staying Current in an Uncertain Future

With these things in mind, there are several ways in which counselors can engage in practices that ensure they provide effective and relevant integrated support. As the circumstances and conditions change over time, there are consistent and sound practices that enable counselors to stay current in an evolving landscape.

Intentional Collaboration

As previously noted, intentional collaboration between counselors focusing on career or mental health offers a mechanism to keep current with ongoing developments in either area. While some may provide an integrated approach, those primarily operating within either domain will benefit from engaging with those operating in a setting that focuses on the corresponding area.

As detailed in this discussion, the dynamic and fluid nature of people's experience with career and mental health makes it challenging to be constantly aware of relevant developments in both domains. Creating a network of providers who address each specific area and are committed to sharing knowledge and resources can assist in staying current. One example is a counselor who focuses on mental health and communicates with community and university career centers about job market trends and skills employers are seeking in applicants.

This information can be used to assist clients who are struggling with employment concerns to not internalize struggles in the job market, which may be impacting their mental health. The client and counselor can develop strategies to attain employment.

Training

In addition to connecting with other providers, it is becoming increasingly important for counselors to engage in professional development focused on an integrated framework. The American Counseling Association, the National Career Development Association, the Society of Vocational Psychology, the International Association of Vocational Education and Guidance, and other organizations have presentations and training focused on integrating career and mental health support. Identifying opportunities to learn about these topics' developments can be instrumental in providing relevant and responsive counseling services.

Measurement of Outcomes

As the future of career and mental health unfolds, measuring counseling outcomes is an essential tool for addressing co-occurring concerns. Selecting measures that evaluate both career and mental health dimensions and their impact within counseling enables a counselor to determine the effectiveness of integrated support. Using career assessments such as the *Career State Inventory* (Leierer et al., 2017), the *Career Thoughts Inventory* (Sampson et al., 1996), the *Self-Directed Search* (Holland & Messer, 2017) paired with various assessments such as the *Session Rating Scale* (Duncan et al., 2003) and the *Penn State Worry Questionnaire* (Molina & Borkovec, 1994) within counseling practice evaluation can provide insight into the impact of counseling services on career development and mental health.

Practitioner-Focused Research

In measuring outcomes, an additional opportunity exists in which practitioner-focused research can be generated. A gap exists between research and practice due to practitioners moving away from evidence-based practice and academic research perceived as having little relevance to the applied world (Islam et al., 2018).

Practitioner-focused research is a means by which systematic evaluation can provide a nimble response to constantly shifting career and mental health conditions. Counseling researchers and practitioners who craft strategies that bridge research and practice while staying attuned to emerging trends will lay the foundation for innovative and transformative approaches. Research facilitated by practitioners in various models, such as program evaluation and single-subject research design, can help demonstrate accountability, evaluate outcomes, and support current practices and procedures (Balkin & Kleist, 2023).

These recommendations equip counselors to adapt to evolving career and mental health trends. While circumstances change rapidly, engaging in these practices keeps counselors informed of developments and provides tools to design effective, responsive integrated interventions.

In this ever-changin' world that brings both opportunities and challenges in career and mental health, counselors are uniquely positioned to serve as valuable resources for individuals navigating this dynamic landscape.

Conclusion

Predicting future events and factors that will impact career development and mental health integration is complicated, as so much is unknown. The trends discussed here offer both challenges and opportunities for career and mental health counseling. Grounding counseling practice in the connection between career, work, and cognitive and affective experiences provides a framework to respond to the shifting conditions that impact well-being. Individualizing services to meet the specific needs of those receiving counseling will enable the counselor to effectively navigate future considerations. Ongoing professional development focused on integrated career and mental health counseling is key to ensuring the counselor responds to relevant pressures on an individual's functioning. In addition, collaboration with other providers, measurement of outcomes, and practitioner-focused research also offer ways to address current and future trends in these domains.

Pro Tips for Providers

- Stay abreast of trends both in career and mental health that are impacting individuals and populations.
- Develop integrated career and mental health interventions that respond to co-occurring career and mental health conditions.

- Engage in counseling training that focuses on career and mental health, with an eye toward current developments in the mental health status of individuals and trends in careers and work.
- Partner with career and mental health-focused counselors to stay aware of evolving conditions.
- Focus on trends in career and explore the impact of these trends on the mental health of those receiving services to mitigate the misattribution of reasons for stress associated with expectations of skills required within the marketplace.
- Attend professional development events and access resources related to career and mental health trends to continually stay informed of effective approaches that account for current career and mental health trends.
- Engage in a systematic evaluation of services combining career and mental health measures to account for the impact of counseling on the dimensions of career and mental health.

Views from the Field

Jon Schlesinger
Executive Director, Hiatt Career Center, Brandeis University

In university career centers, the intersection between career and mental health concerns is an ongoing issue. I see many students describe the internal and external pressures regarding major and career decisions, coupled with the stress and competition of internships, jobs, or graduate school searches. For students accustomed to clear steps from high school to college, the unknown path from a major to a career often surfaces or catalyzes underlying mental health issues.

To support students, our staff onboarding for new career counselors now includes familiarization with common mental health concerns. Training covers the outlines of a mental status exam, basic screening for anxiety and depression, and suicide prevention. Staff also receive ongoing professional development and additional training on working with neurodiverse individuals and students with disabilities. With a focus on first- and second-year students, the career center serves as an early point of contact, providing check-ins on the transition to college when adjustment and academic issues often arise.

The career center builds connections with counseling center partners, including them in professional development sessions and providing tools, resources, and referral guides. Counseling center therapists benefit from understanding career development theories and interventions and generally learning about our work. For instance, a therapist noted that being aware of recruitment timelines helped them better gauge and address a student's anxiety. University career and counseling centers often operate on brief therapy models, highlighting the overlap and shared challenges, especially as many career centers also work with alumni.

The most common mental health concerns I see in the career center include decision-making anxiety and career-related depression. As mental health and disability support grows at the university, we see more students with complex needs, including neurodiverse students, those with processing or executive functioning disabilities, adjustment disorders, family and relationship issues, and trauma. Identity issues also play a greater role in career conversations as students seek roles and companies that reflect their personal values.

I find it productive to work directly with the students to support their mental health issues, acting as a sounding board and additional support rather than working with their therapists. I help students reflect on what they've learned, check in on tasks, and support therapeutic messages, keeping the student at the center of the career process. For example, I worked with "Emma," a recent alumna who had moved back home and was looking for a new job. She disclosed experiences with depression and initial conversations centered around defining career interests. However, anxiety, ADHD issues, and family issues soon overtook career concerns as the primary focus.

As Emma had graduated and worked with multiple therapists, I set boundaries, provided support as she identified new therapists and outpatient programs, and navigated family dynamics. While career remained central, mental health issues frequently resurfaced. I helped her identify and explore career interests with normalization, goal setting, and shared documents. Over several years, I remained a contact point for Emma as she navigated a series of jobs and volunteer opportunities alongside setbacks and conversations with supervisors and parents. My goals were to help her build professional skills and a sense of pride and accomplishment, bolstering her self-efficacy. This ongoing support was necessary as the career and mental health issues were interrelated.

In the career center, we aim to teach students not just to get their first job but to build their careers. Increasingly, those with underlying mental health issues require continued support, necessitating more integration of career and mental health counseling practices to provide a holistic approach for students.

References

Abrams, Z. (2023). AI is changing every aspect of psychology. Here's what to watch for. *Monitor on Psychology*. American Psychological Association. https://www.apa.org/monitor/2023/07/psychology-embracing-ai

Alshabani, N., & Soto, S. (2020). Early 20th-century career counseling for women: Contemporary practice and research implications. *The Career Development Quarterly, 68*(1), 78–93. https://doi.org/10.1002/cdq.12214

Amaral, F. A., Krägeloh, C., Henning, M. A., & Moir, F. (2023). Career indecision, depressive symptoms, self-efficacy and negative thoughts when transitioning from high school: A scoping review. *Australian Journal of Career Development, 32*(2), 158–169. https://doi.org/10.1177/10384162231180339

American College Health Association. (2023). *American College Health Association-National College Health Assessment III: Undergraduate Student Reference Group Executive Summary, Fall 2022*. American College Health Association.

American Counseling Association. (n.d.). *Artificial intelligence in counseling*. https://www.counseling.org/resources/research-reports/artificial-intelligence-counseling

American Counseling Association. (2005). *ACA code of ethics*. https://www.counseling.org/docs/default-source/ethics/archived-code-of-ethics/codeethics05.pdf

American Counseling Association. (2014). *ACA code of ethics*. https://www.counseling.org/docs/default-source/default-document-library/2014-code-of-ethics-finaladdress.pdf

American Psychiatric Association. (2013). *Diagnostic and statistical manual of mental disorders* (5th ed.). https://doi.org/10.1176/appi.books.9780890425596

American Psychiatric Association. (2022). *Diagnostic and statistical manual of mental disorders* (5th ed., text rev.). https://doi.org/10.1176/appi.books.9780890425787

American Psychological Association. (n.d.). *Clinical practice guideline for the treatment of posttraumatic stress disorder.* https://www.apa.org/ptsd-guideline/patients-and-families/cognitive-behavioral

American Psychological Association. (2023). *2023 Work in America Survey.* American Psychological Association. https://www.apa.org/pubs/reports/work-in-america/2023-workplace-health-well-being

American School Counselor Association. (n.d.). *The school counselor and career development.* https://www.schoolcounselor.org/Standards-Positions/Position-Statements/ASCA-Position-Statements/The-School-Counselor-and-Career-Development

American School Counselor Association. (2019). *The ASCA national model: A framework for school counseling programs* (4th ed.).

Amundson, N., Goddard, T., Yoon, H. J., & Niles, S. (2018). Hope-centred interventions with unemployed clients. *The Canadian Journal of Career Development, 17*(2). https://cjcd-rcdc.ceric.ca/index.php/cjcd/article/view/81

Amundson, N. E., Bowlsbey, J. H., & Niles, S. G. (2014). *Essential elements of career counseling: Processes and techniques.* Pearson.

Anctil, T., Klose Smith, C., Schenck, P., & Dahir, C. (2012). Professional school counselors' career development practices and continuing education needs. *Career Development Quarterly, 60*(2), 109–121. https://doi.org/10.1002/j.2161-0045.2012.00009.x

Anderson, W. P., & Niles, S. G. (1995). Career and personal concerns expressed by career counseling clients. *The Career Development Quarterly, 43*(3), 240–245. https://doi.org/10.1002/j.2161-0045.1995.tb00864.x

Arifoulline, N., Milot-Lapointe, F., & Le Corff, Y. (2024). The clinical effects of individual career counseling on clients' psychological distress. *The Career Development Quarterly,* 1–15. https://doi.org/10.1002/cdq.12350

ALGBTIC LGBQQIA Competencies Taskforce. (2013). Association for Lesbian, Gay, Bisexual, and Transgender Issues in counseling competencies for counseling with lesbian, gay, bisexual, queer, questioning, intersex, and ally individuals. *Journal of LGBT Issues in Counseling, 7*(1), 2–43.

Astramovich, R. L., & Coker, J. K. (2007). Program evaluation: The accountability bridge model for counselors. *Journal of Counseling & Development, 85*(2), 162–172. https://doi.org/10.1002/j.1556-6678.2007.tb00459.x

Autin, K. L., Duffy, R. D., Jacobson, C. J., Dosani, K. M., Barker, D., & Bott, E. M. (2018). Career development among undocumented immigrant young adults: A psychology of working perspective. *Journal of Counseling Psychology, 65*(5), 605–617. https://doi.org/10.1037/cou0000280

Balkin, R. S., & Kleist, D. M. (2023). *Counseling research: A practitioner-scholar approach* (2nd ed.). American Counseling Association.

Ballou, M., Balogun, O., Gittens, G., Matsumoto, A., & Sanchez, W. (2015). Trauma and returning to work: Women's lived experiences and its implications for vocational rehabilitation counseling. *Journal of Applied Rehabilitation Counseling, 46*(1), 25–33.

Bandura, A. (1977). Self-efficacy: Toward a unifying theory of behavioral change. *Psychological Review, 84*(2), 191–215. https://doi.org/10.1037/0033-295X.84.2.191

Bandura, A. (1986). *Social foundations of thought and action: A social cognitive theory*. Prentice-Hall.

Beck, A. T. (1993). *Manual for the Beck Hopelessness Scale*. Psychological Corporation.

Beck, A. T., Steer, R. A., & Brown, G. K. (1996). *Beck Depression Inventory–II manual*. Psychological Corporation.

Bernard, J. M. (1979). Supervisor training: A discrimination model. *Counselor Education and Supervision, 19*(1), 60–68. https://doi.org/10.1002/j.1556-6978.1979.tb00906.x

Bernard, J. M. (1997). The discrimination model. In C. E. Watkins Jr. (Ed.), *Handbook of psychotherapy supervision* (pp. 310–327). Wiley.

Betz, N. E., Klein, K. L., & Taylor, K. M. (1996). Evaluation of a short form of the Career Decision-Making Self-Efficacy Scale. *Journal of Career Assessment, 4*(1), 47–57. https://doi.org/10.1177/106907279600400103

Blue Star Families (2024). *Military Family Lifestyle Survey*. https://bluestarfam.org/wp-content/uploads/2024/03/BSF_MFLS_Comp_Infographic_Feb24.pdf

Blustein, D. L. (2006). *The psychology of working: A new perspective for career development, counseling, and public policy*. Routledge.

Blustein, D. L. (2008). The role of work in psychological health and well-being: A conceptual, historical, and public policy perspective. *American Psychologist, 63*(4), 228–240. https://doi.org/10.1037/0003-066X.63.4.228

Blustein, D. L. (2019). *The importance of work in an age of uncertainty: The eroding work experience in America.* Oxford University Press.

Blustein, D. L., Perera, H. N., Diamonti, A. J., Gutowski, E., Meerkins, T., Davila, A., Erby, W., & Konowitz, L. (2020). The uncertain state of work in the U.S.: Profiles of decent work and precarious work. *Journal of Vocational Behavior, 122*, Article 103481. https://doi.org/10.1016/j.jvb.2020.103481

Bright, J. E. H., & Pryor, R. G. L. (2011). The Chaos Theory of Careers. *Journal of Employment Counseling, 48*(4), 163–166. https://doi.org/10.1002/j.2161-1920.2011.tb01104.x

Bronfenbrenner, U. (1979). *The ecology of human development: Experiments by nature and design.* Harvard University Press.

Bruyère, S. M., & Colella, A. (2022). Neurodiversity in the workplace: An overview of interests, issues, and opportunities. In S. M. Bruyère & A. Colella (Eds.), *Neurodiversity in the workplace: Interests, issues, and opportunities* (pp. 1–18). Taylor & Francis.

Bullock-Yowell, E., Andrews, L., & Buzzetta, M. E. (2011). Explaining career decision-making self-efficacy: Personality, cognitions, and cultural mistrust. *The Career Development Quarterly, 59*(5), 400–411. https://doi.org/10.1002/j.2161-0045.2011.tb00967.x

Bullock-Yowell, E., McConnell, A. E., & Schedin, E. A. (2014). Decided and undecided students: Career self-efficacy, negative thinking, and decision-making difficulties. *NACADA Journal, 34*(1), 22–34. https://doi.org/10.12930/NACADA-13-016

Bullock-Yowell, E., Peterson, G. W., Reardon, R. C., Leierer, S. J., & Reed, C. A. (2011). Relationships among career and life stress, negative career thoughts, and career decision state: A cognitive information processing perspective. *The Career Development Quarterly, 59*(4) 302–314. https://doi.org/10.1002/j.2161-0045.2011.tb00071.x

Bullock-Yowell, E., Reed, C. A., Mohn, R. S., Galles, J., Peterson, G. W., & Reardon, R. C. (2015). Neuroticism, negative thinking, and coping with respect to career decision state. *The Career Development Quarterly, 63*(4), 333–347. https://doi.org/10.1002/cdq.12032

Bullock-Yowell, E., Saunders, D. E., & Peterson, G. W. (2015). Thinking about vocational choice. In P. J. Hartung, M. L. Savickas, & W. B.

Walsh (Eds.), *APA handbook of career intervention: Vol. 2. Applications* (pp. 269–281). American Psychological Association. https://doi.org/10.1037/14439-019

Bullock-Yowell, E., & Reardon, R. C. (2024). *Holland's RIASEC Hexagon: A paradigm for life and work decisions.* Florida State Open Publishing. https://doi.org/10.33009/fsop_bullock-yowell0524

Busacca, L. A., & Rehfuss, M. C. (2017). Postmodern career counseling: A new perspective for the 21st century. In L. A. Busacca & M. C. Rehfuss (Eds.), *Postmodern career counseling: A handbook of culture, context, and cases* (pp. 1–19). American Counseling Association.

Buzzetta, M.E., Lenz, J.G., Hayden, S.C.W. and Osborn, D.S. (2020), Student veterans: Meaning in life, negative career thoughts, and depression. *The Career Development Quarterly, 68*(4). 361-373. https://doi.org/10.1002/cdq.12242

Byars-Winston, A., & Rogers, J. G. (2019). Testing intersectionality of race/ethnicity × gender in a social–cognitive career theory model with science identity. *Journal of Counseling Psychology, 66*(1), 30–44. https://doi.org/10.1037/cou0000309

Byun, S. Y., Irvin, M. J., & Meece, J. L. (2015). Rural–non-rural differences in college attendance patterns. *Peabody Journal of Education, 90*(2), 263–279. https://doi.org/10.1080/0161956X.2015.1022384

Cardoso, P., Taveira, M., Biscaia, C., & Santos, G. (2012). Psychologists' dilemmas in career counselling practice. *International Journal for Educational and Vocational Guidance, 12*, 225–241. https://doi.org/10.1007/s10775-012-9232-9

Carlone, H. B., & Johnson, A. (2007). Understanding the science experiences of successful women of color: Science identity as an analytic lens. *Journal of Research in Science Teaching, 44*(8), 1187–1218. https://doi.org/10.1002/tea.20237

Center for Credentialing & Education (n.d.). *GCDF: Global Career Development Facilitator.* https://www.cce-global.org/gcdf

Chan, C. D., Hammer, T. R., Richardson, L., & Hughes, C. L. (2022). Through the relational looking glass: Applications of relational-cultural theory to career development and mental health. *Journal of Employment Counseling, 59*(4), 168–178. https://doi.org/10.1002/joec.12185

Chen, C. P., & Keats, A. (2016). Career development and counselling needs of LGBTQ high school students. *British Journal of Guidance &*

Counselling, 44(5), 576–588. https://doi-org.wake.idm.oclc.org/10.1080/03069885.2016.1187709

Coffey, J., & Lovegrove, E. (2023). More career development learning for neurodivergent tertiary education students: A case study. *Journal of Teaching and Learning for Graduate Employability, 14*(2), 1–15.

Coleman, C. E., Lenz, J. G., & Osborn, D. S. (2023). The relationships among the big 5 personality factors and negative career thoughts. *The Career Development Quarterly, 71,* 30–40. https://doi.org/10.1002/cdq.12313

Conkel-Ziebell, J. L., Gushue, G. V., & Turner, S. L. (2019). Anticipation of racism and sexism: Factors related to setting career goals for urban youth of color. *Journal of Counseling Psychology, 66*(5), 588–599. https://doi.org/10.1037/cou0000357

Costa, P. T., & McCrae, R. R. (2009). The five-factor model and the NEO inventories. In J. N. Butcher (Ed.), *Oxford handbook of personality assessment* (pp. 299–322). Oxford University Press.

Cottone, R. R. (2017). *Theories of counseling and psychotherapy: Individual and relational approaches.* Springer Publishing Company.

Council for Accreditation of Counseling and Related Educational Programs. (2023). *2024 CACREP Standards.* https://www.cacrep.org/wp-content/uploads/2023/06/2024-Standards-Combined-Version-6.27.23.pdf

Crenshaw, K. (2005). Mapping the margins: Intersectionality, identity politics, and violence against women of color (1994). In R. K. Bergen, J. L. Edleson, & C. M. Renzetti (Eds.), *Violence against women: Classic papers* (pp. 282–313). Pearson Education New Zealand.

Crites, J. O. (1976). A comprehensive model of career development in early adulthood. *Journal of Vocational Behavior, 9(1),*105–118.

Cureton, J. L., & Tovey, B. (2023). SHORES: A suicide protective factors tool with applications in career counseling. *The Career Development Quarterly, 71*(2), 124–134. https://doi.org/10.1002/cdq.12317

Currie, J., & Widom, C. S. (2010). Long-term consequences of child abuse and neglect on adult economic well-being. *Child Maltreatment, 15*(2), 111–120. https://doi.org/10.1177/1077559509355316

Das, M., Tang, J., Ringland, K. E., & Piper, A. M. (2021). Towards accessible remote work: Understanding work-from-home practices of neurodivergent professionals. *Proceedings of the ACM on Human-Computer Interaction, 5*(CSCW1), 1–30.

Datti, P. A. (2009). Applying social learning theory of career decision making to gay, lesbian, bisexual, transgender, and questioning young adults. *The Career Development Quarterly, 58*(1), 54–64. https://doi.org/10.1002/j.2161-0045.2009.tb00173.x

Day-Vines, N. L., Wood, S. M., Grothaus, T., Craigen, L., Holman, A., Dotson-Blake, K., & Douglass, M. J. (2016). Broaching the subjects of race, ethnicity, and culture during the counseling process: Erratum. *Journal of Counseling & Development, 94*(1), 123. https://doi.org/10.1002/jcad.12069

Delouya, S. (2023, July). The rise of gig workers is the changing face of the US economy. *CNN.* https://www.cnn.com/2023/07/24/economy/gig-workers-economy-impact-explained/index.html

Diamond, A. (2013). Executive functions. *Annual Review of Psychology, 64,* 135–168. https://doi.org/10.1146/annurev-psych-113011-143750

Dieringer, D. D., Lenz, J. G., Hayden, S. C. W., & Peterson, G. W. (2017). The relation of negative career thoughts to depression and hopelessness. *The Career Development Quarterly, 65*(2), 159–172. https://doi.org/10.1002/cdq.12089

Dipeolu, A. O. (2011). College students with ADHD: Prescriptive concepts for best practices in career development. *Journal of Career Development, 38*(5), 408–427. https://doi.org/10.1177/0894845310378749

Dipeolu, A., Hargrave, S., & Storlie, C. A. (2015). Enhancing ADHD and LD diagnostic accuracy using career instruments. *Journal of Career Development, 42*(1), 19–32. https://doi.org/10.1177/0894845314521691

Doyle, N. (2020). Neurodiversity at work: A biopsychosocial model and the impact on working adults. *British Medical Bulletin, 135*(1), 108–125. https://doi.org/10.1093/bmb/ldaa021

Drake, R. E., & Bond, G. R. (2008). The future of supported employment for people with severe mental illness. *Psychiatric Rehabilitation Journal, 31*(4), 367–376. https://doi.org/10.2975/31.4.2008.367.376

Dreaver, J., Thompson, C., Girdler, S., Adolfsson, M., Black, M. H., & Falkmer, M. (2020). Success factors enabling employment for adults on the autism spectrum from employers' perspective. *Journal of Autism and Developmental Disorders, 50*(5), 1657–1667. https://doi.org/10.1007/s10803-019-03923-3

Duffy, R. D., Blustein, D. L., Diemer, M. A., & Autin, K. L. (2016). The Psychology of Working Theory. *Journal of Counseling Psychology, 63*(2), 127–148. https://doi.org/10.1037/cou0000140

Duffy, R. D., Gensmer, N., Allan, B. A., Kim, H. J., Douglass, R. P., England, J. W., Autin, K. L., & Blustein, D. L. (2019). Developing, validating, and testing improved measures within the Psychology of Working Theory. *Journal of Vocational Behavior, 112*, 199–215. https://doi.org/10.1016/j.jvb.2018.10.012

Duggan, W. (2023). A short history of the Great Recession. *Forbes*. https://www.forbes.com/advisor/investing/great-recession/

Duncan, B. L., Miller, S. D., Sparks, J. A., Calud, D. A., Reynolds, L. R., Brown, J., & Johnson, L. D. (2003). The Session Rating Scale: Preliminary psychometric properties of a working alliance measure. *Journal of Brief Therapy, 3*, 3–12.

El-Hassan, K., & Ghalayini, N. (2020). Parental attachment bonds, dysfunctional career thoughts and career exploration as predictors of career decision-making self-efficacy of Grade 11 students. *British Journal of Guidance & Counselling, 48*(5), 597–610. https://doi.org/10.1080/03069885.2019.1645296

Ellison, M. L., Huckabee, S. S., Stone, R. A., Sabella, K., & Mullen, M. G. (2019). Career services for young adults with serious mental health conditions: Innovations in the field. *The Journal of Behavioral Health Services & Research, 46*, 1–14.

Fisher, L. D., Gushue, G. V., & Cerrone, M. T. (2011). The influences of career support and sexual identity on sexual minority women's career aspirations. *The Career Development Quarterly, 59*(4), 441–454. https://doi.org/10.1002/j.2161-0045.2011.tb00970.x

Flores, L. Y., Ramos, K., & Kanagui, M. (2010). Applying the cultural formulation approach to career counseling with Latinas/os. *Journal of Career Development, 37*(1), 411–422. https://doi.org/10.1177/0894845309345843

Gatesy-Davis, A., Koroloff, N., Marrone, J., & Davis, M. (2022). Collaboration among vocational rehabilitation and mental health leaders: Supporting the vocational success of transition-age youth with serious mental health conditions. *Journal of Vocational Rehabilitation, 56*(2), 123–137. https://doi.org/10.3233/JVR-221177

Gibbons, M. M., Brown, E. C., Daniels, S., Rosecrance, P., Hardin, E. E., & Farrell, I. (2019). Building on strengths while addressing barriers: Career interventions in rural Appalachian communities. *Journal of Career Development, 46*(6), 637–650. https://doi.org/10.1177/0894845319827652

Ginevra, M. C., Nota, L., & Ferrari, L. (2015). Parental support in adolescents' career development: Parents and children's perceptions. *The Career Development Quarterly, 63*(1), 2–15. https://doi.org/10.1002/j.2161-0045.2015.00091.x

Gladding, S. T., & Newsome, D. W. (2018). *Clinical mental health counseling in community and agency settings* (5th ed.). Pearson.

Hagen, J. W., & Hagen, W. W. (1995). What employment counselors need to know about employment discrimination and the Civil Rights Act of 1991. *Journal of Employment Counseling, 32*(1), 2–10. https://doi.org/10.1002/j.2161-1920.1995.tb00419.x

Hanne, K. (2024, June). 24 top AI statistics and trends in 2024. *Forbes.* https://www.forbes.com/advisor/business/ai-statistics/

Hansen, J. T. (2006). Counseling theories within a postmodernist epistemology: New roles for theories in counseling practice. *Journal of Counseling & Development, 84*(3), 291–297. https://doi.org/10.1002/j.1556-6678.2006.tb00408.x

Hartung, P. J. (2015). The career construction interview. In M. McMahon & M. Watson (Eds.), *Career assessment. Career development series* (pp. 189–203). SensePublishers. https://doi.org/10.1007/978-94-6300-034-5_13

Hartung, P. J., & Blustein, D. L. (2002). Reason, intuition, and social justice: Elaborating on Parsons's career decision-making model. *Journal of Counseling & Development, 80*(1), 41–47. https://doi.org/10.1002/j.1556-6678.2002.tb00164.x

Hayden, S. C. W. (2019). Innovative utilization of the discrimination model for career-focused counseling supervision. In J. G. Maree (Ed.), *Handbook of innovative career counselling* (pp. 89–101). Springer. https://doi.org/10.1007/978-3-030-22799-9_6

Hayden, S., & Kronholz, J. (2015). Integration of assessments in counseling: Developing competence within clinical supervision. *Career Planning and Adult Development Journal, 30*(4), 156–169.

Hayden, S. C. W., Kronholz, J., Pawley, E., & Theall, K. (2016). Major depressive disorder and career development: Link and implications. *Career Planning and Adult Development Journal, 32*(1), 19–31.

Hayden, S. C. W., Osborn, D. S., & Costello, K. (2023). The connection between executive processing and career development. *Journal of the National Institute for Career Education and Counselling, 50*(1), 29–40. https://doi.org/10.20856/jnicec.5004

Hayden, S. C. W., Osborn, D. S., Peace, C., & Lange, R. (2021). Enhancing agency in career development via cognitive information processing theory. *British Journal of Guidance & Counselling, 49*(2), 304–315. https://doi.org/10.1080/03069885.2020.1867703

Hayes, S. C. (2023, August). What the future of mental health care looks like. *Psychology Today.* https://www.psychologytoday.com/us/blog/get-out-of-your-mind/202308/what-the-future-of-mental-health-care-looks-like

Hays, D. G. (2024). *Assessment in counseling: Procedures and practices* (7th ed.). American Counseling Association.

Herr, E. L. (2013). Trends in the history of vocational guidance. *The Career Development Quarterly, 61*(3), 277–282. https://doi.org/10.1002/j.2161-0045.2013.00056.x

Hershenson, D. B. (2008). A head of its time: Career counseling's roots in phrenology. *The Career Development Quarterly, 57*(2), 181–190. https://doi.org/10.1002/j.2161-0045.2008.tb00046.x

Hetherington, C. (1991). Life planning and career counseling with gay and lesbian students. In N. J. Evans & V. A. Wall (Eds.), *Beyond tolerance: Gays, lesbians, and bisexuals on campus* (pp. 131–145). American College Personnel Association.

Hines, E. M., & Owen, L. (Eds.). (2022). *Equity-based career development and postsecondary transitions: An American imperative.* Information Age Publishing.

Hinkelman, J. M., & Luzzo, D. A. (2007). Mental health and career development of college students. *Journal of Counseling & Development, 85*(2), 143–147. https://doi.org/10.1002/j.1556-6678.2007.tb00456.x

Hoff, K. A., Song, Q. C., Wee, C. J., Phan, W. M. J., & Rounds, J. (2020). Interest fit and job satisfaction: A systematic review and meta-analysis. *Journal of Vocational Behavior, 123*, 103503. https://doi.org/10.1016/j.jvb.2020.10350

Hooley, T., Pearcy, C., & Neary, S. (2023). Investing in careers: What is career guidance worth? *Career Development Policy Group.* https://adventuresincareerdevelopment.wordpress.com/2023/07/18/investing-in-careers-what-is-career-guidance-worth/

Holland, J. L. (1959). A theory of vocational choice. *Journal of Counseling Psychology, 6*(1), 35–45.

Holland, J. L., Daiger, D., & Power, P. (1980). *My Vocational Situation.* Consulting Psychologists Press.

Holland, J. L., & Messer, M. A. (2017). *Self-directed search.* Psychological Assessment Resources.

Holland, J. L., & Messer, M. A. (2017). *Standard SDS assessment booklet*. Psychological Assessment Resources.

Howard, K. A., Flanagan, S., Castine, E., & Walsh, M. E. (2015). Perceived influences on the career choices of children and youth: An exploratory study. *International Journal for Vocational and Educational Guidance, 15*, 99–111.

Howard, M. C., Follmer, K. B., Smith, M. B., Tucker, R. P., & Van Zandt, E. C. (2021). Work and suicide: An interdisciplinary systematic literature review. *Journal of Organizational Behavior, 43*(2), 1–26. https://doi.org/10.1002/job.2519

In-Work Project. (n.d.). *In-Work Project*. https://www.in-work-project.eu/english/

Islam, S., Chetta, M. H., Martins, A., van Govan, D., Kozikowski, A., & Needhammer, J. (2018). The scientist–practitioner gap among master's level I-O psychology practitioners: A text-analytic exploration. *Industrial-Organizational Psychologist, 55*(3). https://touroscholar.touro.edu/dbs_pubs/47

Ivanovic, A. (2023). Career advancement barriers faced by LGBTQ employees: An exploration of discrimination, bias, and inclusion in the workplace. *Reviews of Contemporary Business Analytics, 6*(1), 43–56. https://researchberg.com/index.php/rcba/article/view/116

Jemini-Gashi, L., Duraku, Z. H., & Kelmendi, K. (2021). Associations between social support, career self-efficacy, and career indecision among youth. *Current Psychology, 40*, 4691–4697. https://doi.org/10.1007/s12144-019-00402-x

Jia, Y., Hou, Z.-J., Zhang, H., & Xiao, Y. (2022). Future time perspective, career adaptability, anxiety, and career decision-making difficulty: Exploring mediations and moderations. *Journal of Career Development, 49*(2), 282–296. https://doi.org/10.1177/0894845320941922

Jiang, Z. (2014). Emotional intelligence and career decision-making self-efficacy: National and gender differences. *Journal of Employment Counseling, 51*, 112–124. https://doi.org/10.1002/j.2161-1920.2014.00046.x

Jo, H., Ra, Y.-A., Lee, J., & Kim, W. H. (2016). Impact of dysfunctional career thoughts on career decision self-efficacy and vocational identity. *The Career Development Quarterly, 64*, 333–344. https://doi.org/10.1002/cdq.12069

Joon Yoon, H., In, H., Niles, S. G., Amundson, N. E., Smith, B. A., & Mills, L. (2015). The effects of hope on student engagement, academic performance, and vocational identity. *Canadian Journal of Career Development, 14*(1), 34–45. https://cjcd-rcdc.ceric.ca/index.php/cjcd/article/view/176

Jones, L. K. (1994). Frank Parsons' contribution to career counseling. *Journal of Career Development, 20*(4), 287–294. https://doi.org/10.1177/089484539402000403

Kang, H. J., Callahan, J. L., & Anne, M. (2015). An intersectional social capital model of career development for international marriage immigrants. *The Career Development Quarterly, 63*(3), 238–252. https://doi.org/10.1002/cdq.12016

Kaplan, D. M., Tarvydas, V. M., & Gladding, S. T. (2014). 20/20: A vision for the future of counseling: The new consensus definition of counseling. *Journal of Counseling & Development, 92*(3), 366–372.

Kaufmann, C. (2008). ILO, declaration on social justice for a fair globalization. *International Labor Organization*.

Kenny, M. E., & Di Fabio, A. (2009). Prevention and career development. *Risorsa Uomo: Rivista di Psicologia del Lavoro e dell' Organizzazione, 15*(4), 361–374.

Kılavuz, T., & İnandı, Y. (2022). The relationship of the career barriers of women teachers with their perceptions of professional social support and hopelessness level: Evidence from Turkey. *International Journal of Leadership in Education, 25*(6). https://doi.org/10.1080/13603124.2022.2098380

Koçak, O., Ak, N., Erdem, S. S., Sinan, M., Younis, M. Z., & Erdoğan, A. (2021). The role of family influence and academic satisfaction on career decision-making self-efficacy and happiness. *International Journal of Environmental Research and Public Health, 18*(11), 5919. https://doi.org/10.3390/ijerph18115919

Koricich, A., Chen, X., & Hughes, R. P. (2018). Understanding the effects of rurality and socioeconomic status on college attendance and institutional choice in the United States. *The Review of Higher Education, 41*(2), 281–305. https://doi.org/10.1353/rhe.2018.0004

Kosciw, J. G., Greytak, E. A., Palmer, N. A., & Boesen, M. J. (2014). *The 2013 National School Climate Survey: The experiences of lesbian, gay, bisexual and transgender youth in our nation's schools*. GLSEN.

Krumboltz, J. D. (1993). Integrating career and personal counseling. *The Career Development Quarterly, 42*(2), 143–147. https://doi.org/10.1002/j.2161-0045.1993.tb00427.x

Krumboltz, J. D. (2009). The happenstance learning theory. *Journal of Career Assessment, 17*(2), 135–154. https://doi.org/10.1177/1069072708328861

Krumboltz, J. D., Mitchell, A. M., & Jones, G. B. (1976). A social learning theory of career selection. *The Counseling Psychologist, 6*(1), 71–81. https://doi.org/10.1177/001100007600600117

Lara, T. M., Kline, W. B., & Paulson, D. (2011). Attitudes regarding career counseling: Perceptions and experiences of counselors-in-training. *The Career Development Quarterly, 59*, 428–440. https://doi.org/10.1002/j.2161-0045.2011.tb00969.x

Lawson, G., & Myers, J. E. (2011). Wellness, professional quality of life, and career-sustaining behaviors: What keeps us well? *Journal of Counseling & Development, 89*(2), 163–171. https://doi.org/10.1002/j.1556-6678.2011.tb00074.x

Leierer, S. J., Peterson, G. W., Reardon, R. C., & Saunders, D. E. (2010). Connecting career and mental health counseling: Integrating theory and practice. *VISTAS Online*. http://counselingoutfitters.com/vistas/vistas10/Article_01.pdf

Leierer, S. J., Peterson, G. W., Reardon, R. C., & Osborn, D. S. (2017). *The Career State Inventory (CSI) as a measure of readiness for career decision making: A manual for assessment, administration, and intervention 7.0* (Technical Report No. 57). Florida State University. http://purl.flvc.org/fsu/fd/FSU_libsubv1_scholarship_submission_1517522495_ad48ff10

Leierer, S. J., Wilde, C. K., Peterson, G. W., & Reardon, R. C. (2016). The career decision state and rehabilitation counselor education programs. *Rehabilitation Counseling Bulletin, 59*(3), 133–142. https://doi.org/10.1177/0034355215579278

Lent, R. W. (2005). A social cognitive view of career development and counseling. In S. D. Brown & R. W. Lent (Eds.), *Career development and counseling: Putting theory and research to work* (pp. 101–127). New York, NY: Wiley.

Lent, R. W. (2013). Career-life preparedness: Revisiting career planning and adjustment in the new workplace. *The Career Development Quarterly, 61*(1), 2–14. https://doi.org/10.1002/j.2161-0045.2013.00031.x

Lent, R. W., & Brown, S. D. (2008). Social cognitive career theory and subjective well-being in the context of work. *Journal of Career Assessment, 16*(1), 6–21. https://doi.org/10.1177/1069072707305769

Lent, R. W., & Brown, S. D. (2019). Social cognitive career theory at 25: Empirical status of the interest, choice, and performance models. *Journal of Vocational Behavior, 115*, 103316. https://doi.org/10.1016/j.jvb.2019.06.004

Lent, R. W., Brown, S. D., & Hackett, G. (1994). Toward a unifying social cognitive theory of career and academic interest, choice, and performance. *Journal of Vocational Behavior, 45*, 79–122.

Lenz, J. G., Peterson, G. W., Reardon, R. C., & Saunders, D. (2010). Connecting career and mental health counseling. *VISTAS Online Journal*, 1-16.

Leong, F. T. L., Hardin, E., & Gupta, A. (2007). Culture and self in vocational psychology: A cultural formulations approach to career assessment and career counseling. *Conference of the Society for Vocational Psychology of the American Psychological Association*, Akron, OH.

Luke, J., Bartlett, C., March, S., & McIlveen, P. (2024). A systematic review of effective local, community, or peer-delivered interventions to improve well-being and employment in regional, rural, and remote areas of Australia. *The Australian Journal of Rural Health, 32*(3), 433–454. https://doi.org/10.1111/ajr.13113

Lupton-Smith, H., Peterssen, K., & Smith, A. C. (2024). Career counseling settings across the lifespan. In A. C. Smith & K. Peterssen (Eds.), *An innovative approach to career counseling*. Springer Publishing.

Luzzo, D. A., & McWhirter, E. H. (2001). Sex and ethnic differences in the perception of educational and career-related barriers and levels of coping efficacy. *Journal of Counseling & Development, 79*(1), 61–67. https://doi.org/10.1002/j.1556-6676.2001.tb01944.x

Mahmud, M. S., Talukder, M. U., & Rahman, S. M. (2021). Does 'fear of COVID-19' trigger future career anxiety? An empirical investigation considering depression from COVID-19 as a mediator. *The International Journal of Social Psychiatry, 67*(1), 35–45. https://doi.org/10.1177/0020764020935488

McAuliffe, G. J. (1992). Assessing and changing career decision-making self-efficacy expectations. *Journal of Career Development, 19*(1), 25–36.

McCartney, P., & McCartney, L. (1973). *Live and let die* [Song]. On *Live and Let Die*. United Artists.

McDowall, A., Doyle, N., & Kiseleva, M. (2023). Neurodiversity at work: Demand, supply and a gap analysis. Birkbeck University of London.

References

McDowell, C., Fossey, E., & Harvey, C. (2022). Moving clients forward: A grounded theory of disability employment specialists' views and practices. *Disability and Rehabilitation: An International, Multidisciplinary Journal, 44*(19), 5504–5512. https://doi.org/10.1080/09638288.2021.1937341

McIlveen, P. (2015). Psychotherapy, counseling, and career counseling. In P. J. Hartung, M. L. Savickas, & W. B. Walsh (Eds.), *APA handbook of career intervention, Vol. 1: Foundations* (pp. 403–417). American Psychological Association. https://doi.org/10.1037/14438-022

McKay, H., Bright, J. E. H., & Pryor, R. G. L. (2005). Finding order and direction from chaos: A comparison of chaos career counseling and trait matching counseling. *Journal of Employment Counseling, 42*(3), 98–112.

Merriam-Webster. (n.d.). *BIPOC*. https://www.merriam-webster.com/dictionary/BIPOC

Metheny, J., & McWhirter, E. H. (2013). Contributions of social status and family support to college students' career decision self-efficacy and outcome expectations. *Journal of Career Assessment, 21*(3), 378–394. https://doi.org/10.1177/1069072712475164

Miller, W. R., & Rollnick, S. (2023). *Motivational interviewing: Helping people change* (4th ed.). Guilford Press.

Molina, S., & Borkovec, T. D. (1994). The Penn State Worry Questionnaire: Psychometric properties and associated characteristics. In G. C. L. Davey & F. Tallis (Eds.), *Worrying: Perspectives on theory, assessment and treatment* (pp. 265–283). John Wiley & Sons.

Moothedan, E., Katoju, S., Nguyen, O. T., Faldu, A., Motwani, K., & Feller, D. B. (2024). Patient-level factors associated with referral rates to mental health services in a network of student-run free clinics: A pooled cross-sectional study. *Journal of Student-Run Clinics, 10*(1). https://doi.org/10.59586/jsrc.v10i1.417

Morales, D. A., Barksdale, C. L., & Beckel-Mitchener, A. C. (2020). A call to action to address rural mental health disparities. *Journal of Clinical and Translational Science, 4*(5), 463–467. https://doi.org/10.1017/cts.2020.42

Mowreade, A. (2023, November). Health apps serve as student wellness maps. *Insider Higher Ed*. https://www.insidehighered.com/news/student-success/healthwellness/2023/11/15/universities-use-apps-provide-health-education#

Mulvaney-Day, N., Dean, D., Jr., Miller, K., & Camacho-Cook, J. (2022). Trends in use of telehealth for behavioral health care during the COVID-19 pandemic: Considerations for payers and employers. *American Journal of Health Promotion, 36*(7), 1237–1241. https://doi.org/10.1177/08901171221112488e

Murray, C. E. (2009). Diffusion of innovation theory: A bridge for the research-practice gap in counseling. *Journal of Counseling & Development, 87*, 108–116. https://doi.org/10.1002/j.1556-6678.2009.tb00556.x

Murray, N., Hatfield, M., Falkmer, M., & Falkmer, T. (2016). Evaluation of career planning tools for use with individuals with autism spectrum disorder: A systematic review. *Research in Autism Spectrum Disorders, 23*, 188–202. https://doi.org/10.1016/j.rasd.2015.12.007

Myers, J. E., & Sweeney, T. J. (2004). The Indivisible Self: An evidence-based model of wellness. *Journal of Individual Psychology, 60*(3), 234–245.

National Career Development Association. (n.d.-a). *About history*. https://ncda.org/aws/NCDA/pt/sp/about_history

National Career Development Association. (n.d.-b). *Credentialing*. https://ncda.org/aws/NCDA/pt/sp/credentialing_home_page

National Career Development Association. (2024a). *NCDA 2024 code of ethics*. Author. https://www.ncda.org/aws/NCDA/asset_manager/get_file/3395

National Career Development Association. (2024b). *Membership report*. https://ncda.org/aws/NC

Nauta, M. M. (2010). The development, evolution, and status of Holland's theory of vocational personalities: Reflections and future directions for counseling psychology. *Journal of Counseling Psychology, 57*(1), 11–22. https://doi.org/10.1037/a0018213

Niles, S., Amundson, N., & Neault, R. (2011). *Career flow: A hope-centered approach to career development*. Pearson Merrill Prentice Hall.

Niles, S. G., & Harris-Bowlsbey, J. (2022). *Career development interventions for the 21st century* (6th ed.). Pearson.

Niles, S. G., In, H., & Amundson, N. E. (2014). Using an action-oriented, hope-centered model of career development. *Journal of Asia Pacific Counseling, 4*, 1–13.

Niles, S. G., & Karajic, A. (2008). Training career practitioners in the 21st century. In J. A. Athanasou & R. van Esbroeck (Eds.), *International handbook of career guidance* (pp. 355–374). Springer.

Niles, S. G., Yoon, H. J., & Amundson, N. E. (2010). *The Hope-Centered Career Inventory* [Online assessment]. http://mycareerflow.com

Novakovic, A., Patrikakou, E. N., & Ockerman, M. S. (2021). School counselor perceptions of preparation and importance of college and career readiness counseling. *Professional School Counseling, 25*(1). https://doi.org/10.1177/2156759X21998391

Nye, A., Delgadillo, J., & Barkham, M. (2023). Efficacy of personalized psychological interventions: A systematic review and meta-analysis. *Journal of Consulting and Clinical Psychology, 91*(7), 389–397. https://doi.org/10.1037/ccp0000820

O'Brien, K. M. (2001). The legacy of Parsons: Career counselors and vocational psychologists as agents of social change. *The Career Development Quarterly, 50*(1), 66–76. https://doi.org/10.1002/j.2161-0045.2001.tb00891.x

Ockerman, M. S., Patrikakou, E., & Novakovic, A. (2023). Fostering continuity in college and career counseling K–12: Training and perceived confidence between K–8 and high school counselors. *Professional School Counseling, 27*(1). https://doi.org/10.1177/2156759X231190328

Osborn, D. S., & Dames, L. S. (2013). Teaching graduate career classes: A national survey of career instructors. *Counselor Education and Supervision, 52*(4), 297–310.

Osborn, D. S., Hayden, S. C., Marks, L. R., Hyatt, T., Saunders, D., & Sampson, J. P. (2022). Career practitioners' response to career development concerns in the time of COVID-19. *The Career Development Quarterly, 70*(1), 52–66. https://doi.org/10.1002/cdq.12283

Osborn, D. S., Hayden, S. W., Peterson, G. W., & Sampson Jr., J. P. (2016). Effect of brief staff-assisted career service delivery on drop-in clients. *The Career Development Quarterly, 64*, 181–187. https://doi.org/10.1002/cdq.12050

Osborn, D. S., Kronholz, J. F., & Finklea, J. T. (2015). Card sorts. In M. McMahon & M. Watson (Eds.), *Career assessment: Qualitative approaches* (pp. 123–141). Springer.

Osborn, D. S., Sides, R. D., & Brown, C. B. (2020). Comparing career development outcomes for undergraduate CIP-based courses versus human relations courses. *The Career Development Quarterly, 68*(1), 32–47. https://doi.org/10.1002/cdq.12211

Pager, D., & Pedulla, D. S. (2015). Race, self-selection, and the job search process. *American Journal of Sociology, 120*(4), 1005–1054. https://doi.org/10.1086/681072

Parmentier, M., Pirsoul, T., & Nils, F. (2019). Examining the impact of emotional intelligence on career adaptability: A two-wave cross-lagged study. *Personality and Individual Differences, 151*(1), 109446. https://doi.org/10.1016/j.paid.2019.05.052

Park, K., Woo, S., Park, K., Kyea, J., & Yang, E. (2017). The mediation effects of career exploration on the relationship between trait anxiety and career indecision. *Journal of Career Development, 44*(5), 440–452. https://doi.org/10.1177/0894845316662346

Parsons, F. (1909). *Choosing a vocation*. Houghton Mifflin.

Pearson Assessments. (n.d.). *Qualifications policies*. https://www.pearsonassessments.com/professional-assessments/ordering/how-to-order/qualifications/qualifications-policy.html

Pesce, N. L. (2019, April 2). Most college grads with autism can't find jobs. This group is fixing that. *MarketWatch*. https://www.marketwatch.com/story/most-college-grads-with-autism-cant-find-jobs-this-group-is-fixing-that-2017-04-10-5881421

Petrie, K., Joyce, S., Tan, L., Henderson, M., Johnson, A., Nguyen, H., Modini, M., Groth, M., Glozier, N., & Harvey, S. (2018). A framework to create more mentally healthy workplaces: A viewpoint. *Australian & New Zealand Journal of Psychiatry, 52*(1), 15–23. https://doi.org/10.1177/0004867417726174

Peterson, G., Lenz, J. G., & Osborn, D. S. (2016). *Decision Space Worksheet (DSW) Activity Manual*. https://career.fsu.edu/sites/g/files/upcbnu746/files/files/tech-center/resources/service-delivery-handouts/DSWActivityManual_RevAug2016.pdf

Pew Research Center. (2024, January). *Mobile fact sheet*. https://www.pewresearch.org/internet/fact-sheet/mobile/

Pope, M. (2000). A brief history of career counseling in the United States. *Career Development Quarterly, 48*(3), 194–211. https://doi.org/10.1002/j.2161-0045.2000.tb00286.x

Pordelan, N., & Hosseinian, S. (2021). Online career counseling success: The role of hardiness and psychological capital. *International Journal for Educational and Vocational Guidance, 21*(3), 531–549. https://doi.org/10.1007/s10775-020-09452-1

Powers, J. J., & Duys, D. (2020). Toward trauma-informed career counseling. *The Career Development Quarterly, 68*(2), 173–185. https://doi.org/10.1002/cdq.12221

Prescod, D. J., & Zeligman, M. (2018). Career adaptability of trauma survivors: The moderating role of posttraumatic growth. *The Career Development Quarterly, 66*(2), 107–120. https://doi.org/10.1002/cdq.12126

Pryor, R. G. L., & Bright, J. E. H. (2003a). The chaos theory of careers. *Australian Journal of Career Development, 12*(2), 12–20.

Pryor, R. G. L., & Bright, J. E. H. (2003b). Order and chaos: A twenty-first century formulation of careers. *Australian Journal of Psychology, 55*, 121–128.

Pryor, R. G. L., & Bright, J. E. H. (2011). *The chaos theory of careers*. Routledge.

Raymund, P., Garcia, J. M., Restubog, S. L. D., Bordia, P., Bordia, S., & Roxas, R. E. O. (2015). Career optimism: The roles of contextual support and career decision-making self-efficacy. *Journal of Vocational Behavior, 88*, 10–18. https://doi.org/10.1016/j.jvb.2015.02.004

Reardon, R. C., Lenz, J. G., Peterson, G. P., & Sampson, J. P. (2023). *Career development and planning: A comprehensive approach* (7th ed.). Kendall Hunt.

Redekopp, D. E., & Huston, M. (2019). The broader aims of career development: Mental health, well-being, and work. *British Journal of Guidance & Counselling, 47*(2), 246–257. https://doi.org/10.1080/03069885.2018.1513451

Reinert, M., Fritze, D., & Nguyen, T. (2022, October). The state of mental health in America 2023. *Mental Health America*.

Restubog, S. L. D., Florentino, A. R., & Garcia, P. R. J. M. (2010). The mediating roles of career self-efficacy and career decidedness in the relationship between contextual support and persistence. *Journal of Vocational Behavior, 77*(2), 186–195. https://doi.org/10.1016/j.jvb.2010.06.005

Robertson, P. J. (2013). Career guidance and public mental health. *International Journal for Educational and Vocational Guidance, 13*(2), 151–164. https://doi.org/10.1007/s10775-013-9246-y

Rojewski, J. W. (2006). Career education. In J. H. Greenhaus & G. A. Callanan (Eds.), *Encyclopedia of career development*. Sage Publications. https://doi.org/10.4135/9781412952675.n40

Rollins, J. (2021, January). The forces that could shape counseling's future. *Counseling Today*. https://www.counseling.org/publications/counseling-today-magazine/article-archive/article/legacy/the-forces-that-could-shape-counselings-future

Rottinghaus, P. J., Jenkins, N., & Jantzer, A. M. (2009). Relation of depression and affectivity to career decision status and self-efficacy in college students. *Journal of Career Assessment, 17*(3), 271–285. https://doi.org/10.1177/1069072708330463

Rutledge, M. L., & Gnilka, P. B. (2022). Breaking down barriers: A culturally responsive career development intervention with racially minoritized girls of color. *Journal of College Access, 7*(1), 7.

Sampson, J. P., Jr., Dozier, V. C., & Colvin, G. P. (2011). Translating career theory to practice: The risk of unintentional social injustice. *Journal of Counseling & Development, 89*(3), 326–337.

Sampson, J. P., Jr., & Lenz, J. G. (2023). *Designing and implementing career interventions: A handbook for effective practice* (2nd ed.). National Career Development Association.

Sampson, J. P., Jr., Lenz, J. G., Bullock-Yowell, E., Osborn, D. S., & Hayden, S. C. W. (2023). *Cognitive information processing theory: Career theory, research, and practice*. Florida State Open Publishing. https://doi.org/10.33009/fsop_sampson1123

Sampson, J. P., McClain, M. C., Musch, E., & Reardon, R. C. (2017). The supply and demand for career development programs and services as a social justice issue. In V. S. H. Solberg & S. R. Ali (Eds.), *Handbook of career and workforce development research, practice, and policy* (pp. 57–75). Routledge. https://doi.org/10.4324/9781315714769-4

Sampson, J. P., Osborn, D. S., Bullock-Yowell, E., Lenz, J. G., Peterson, G. W., Dozier, V. C., Leierer, S. J., Hayden, S. C. W., & Saunders, D. E. (2020). *An introduction to cognitive information processing theory, research, and practice*. Florida State University, Center for the Study of Technology in Counseling and Career Development. http://purl.flvc.org/fsu/fd/FSU_libsubv1_scholarship_submission_1593091156_c171f50a

Sampson, J. P., Jr., Peterson, G. W., Lenz, J. G., Reardon, R. C., & Saunders, D. E. (1996a). *Career thoughts inventory*. PAR.

Sampson, J. P., Jr., Peterson, G. W., Lenz, J. G., Reardon, R. C., & Saunders, D. E. (1996b). *Career thoughts inventory: Professional manual*. PAR.

Sampson, J. P., Jr., Reardon, R. C., Peterson, G. W., & Lenz, J. G. (2004). *Career counseling and services: A cognitive information processing approach*. Brooks/Cole.

Saunders, D. E., Peterson, G. W., Sampson, J. P., Jr., & Reardon, R. C. (2000). Relationship of depression and dysfunctional career thinking to career indecision. *Journal of Vocational Behavior, 56*, 288–298.

Savickas, M. L. (2003). Advancing the career counseling profession: Objectives and strategies for the next decade. *The Career Development Quarterly, 52*(1), 87–96. https://doi.org/10.1002/j.2161-0045.2003.tb00631.x

Savickas, M. L. (2011). *Career counseling*. American Psychological Association.

Savickas, M. L., Nota, L., Rossier, J., Dauwalder, J., Duarte, M. E., Guichard, J., Soresi, S., Van Esbroeck, R., & van Vianen, A. E. M. (2009). Life designing: A paradigm for career construction in the 21st century. *Journal of Vocational Behavior, 75*(3), 239–250. https://doi.org/10.1016/j.jvb.2009.04.004

Schmidt, C. K., & Nilsson, J. E. (2006). The effects of simultaneous developmental processes: Factors relating to the career development of lesbian, gay, and bisexual youth. *The Career Development Quarterly, 55*(1), 22–33. https://doi.org/10.1002/j.2161-0045.2006.tb00003.x

Shen-Miller, D. S., McWhirter, E. H., & Bartone, A. S. (2012). Historical influences on the evolution of vocational counseling. In D. Capuzzi & M. D. Stauffer (Eds.), *Career counseling: Foundations, perspectives, and applications* (2nd ed., pp. 3–42). Routledge/Taylor & Francis Group.

Sheu, H. B. (2023). Temporal precedence between and mediating effects of career decision self-efficacy and career exploratory behavior among first-year college students: Within-person and between-person analyses by race/ethnicity and gender. *Journal of Vocational Behavior, 144*, 103882. https://doi.org/10.1016/j.jvb.2023.103882

Showalter, D., Hartman, S. L., Johnson, J., & Klein, B. (2019). Why rural matters 2018-2019: The time is now. *A report of the Rural School and Community Trust*. Rural School and Community Trust.

Slaney, R. B. (1978). Expressed and inventoried vocational interests: A comparison of instruments. *Journal of Counseling Psychology, 25*(6), 520–529. https://doi.org/10.1037/0022-0167.25.6.520

Slaney, R. B. (1980). Expressed vocational choice and vocational indecision. *Journal of Counseling Psychology, 27*(2), 122–129. https://doi.org/10.1037/0022-0167.27.2.122

Smith, A. C., & Peterssen, K. (2024). Career: Defining and highlighting the journey. In A. C. Smith & K. Peterssen (Eds.), *An innovative approach to career counseling*. Springer Publishing.

Smith, B. A., Mills, L., Amundson, N. E., Niles, S., & In, H. (2014). What helps and hinders the hopefulness of post-secondary students who have experienced significant barriers. *Canadian Journal of Career Development, 13*(2), 59–74. https://cjcd-rcdc.ceric.ca/index.php/cjcd/article/view/183

Sparks, D. M. (2017). Navigating STEM-worlds: Applying a lens of intersectionality to the career identity development of underrepresented female students of color. *Journal for Multicultural Education, 11*(3), 162–175.

Stebleton, M. J., & Eggerth, D. E. (2012). Returning to our roots: Immigrant populations at work. *Journal of Career Development, 39*(1), 3–12. https://doi.org/10.1177/0894845311417131

Steger, M. F., Frazier, P., Oishi, S., & Kaler, M. (2006). The Meaning in Life Questionnaire: Assessing the presence of and search for meaning in life. *Journal of Counseling Psychology, 53*(1), 80–93. https://doi.org/10.1037/0022-0167.53.1.80

Stoltz, K. B., Wolff, L. A., & McClelland, S. S. (2011). Exploring lifestyle as a predictor of career adaptability using a predominantly African American rural sample. *Journal of Individual Psychology, 67*(2).

Super, D. E. (1963). Self-concepts in vocational development. In D. E. Super, R. Stariskevsky, N. Matlin, & J. P. Jordaan (Eds.), *Career development: Self-concept theory* (pp. 1–26). College Entrance Examination Board.

Super, D. E. (1980). A life-span, life-space approach to career development. *Journal of Vocational Behavior, 16*, 282–298. https://doi.org/10.1016/0001-8791(80)90056-1

Super, D. E. (1990). A life-span, life-space approach to career development. In D. Brown & L. Brooks (Eds.), *Career choice and development: Applying contemporary theories to practice* (2nd ed., pp. 197–261). Jossey-Bass.

Super, D. E. (1996). A life-span, life-space approach to career development. In D. Brown, L. Brooks, & Associates (Eds.), *Career choice and development* (3rd ed., pp. 197–245). Jossey-Bass.

Super, D. E., Savickas, M. L., & Super, C. M. (1996). The life-span, life-space approach to careers. In D. Brown & L. Brooks (Eds.), *Career choice and development* (3rd ed., pp. 121–178). Jossey-Bass.

Symington, A. (2004). Intersectionality: A tool for gender and economic justice. *Women's Rights and Economic Change, 9*, 1–8.

Szulc, J. M., Davies, J., Tomczak, M. T., & McGregor, F.-L. (2021). AMO perspectives on the well-being of neurodivergent human capital. *Employee Relations, 43*(4), 858–872. https://doi.org/10.1108/ER-09-2020-0446

Szulc, J. M., McGregor, F.-L., & Cakir, E. (2023). Neurodiversity and remote work in times of crisis: Lessons for HR. *Personnel Review, 52*(6), 1677–1692.

Takil, N. B., & Sari, B. A. (2021). Trait anxiety vs career anxiety in relation to attentional control. *Current Psychology: A Journal for Diverse Perspectives on Diverse Psychological Issues, 40*(5), 2366–2370. https://doi.org/10.1007/s12144-019-0169-8

Tang, M., Montgomery, M. L. T., Collins, B., & Jenkins, K. (2021). Integrating career and mental health counseling: Necessity and strategies. *Journal of Employment Counseling, 58*(1), 23–35. https://doi.org/10.1002/joec.12155

Taylor, K. M., & Betz, N. E. (1983). Applications of self-efficacy theory to the understanding and treatment of career indecision. *Journal of Vocational Behavior, 22*(1), 63–81. https://doi.org/10.1016/0001-8791(83)90006-4

Thompson, M. N., Her, P., Fetter, A. K., & Perez-Chavez, J. (2019). College student psychological distress: Relationship to self-esteem and career decision self-efficacy beliefs. *The Career Development Quarterly, 67*, 282–297. https://doi.org/10.1002/cdq.12199

Thouin, É., Dupéré, V., & Denault, A. S. (2023). Paid employment in adolescence and rapid integration into a career-related job in early adulthood among vulnerable youth: The identity connection. *Journal of Vocational Behavior, 142*, 103864. https://doi.org/10.1016/j.jvb.2023.103864

Tovar-Murray, D., Jenifer, E. S., Andrusyk, J., D'Angelo, R., & King, T. (2012). Racism-related stress and ethnic identity as determinants of African American college students' career aspirations. *Career Development Quarterly, 60*(3), 254–262. https://doi.org/10.1002/j.2161-0045.2012.00021.x

United States Census Bureau. (2016). New census data show differences between urban and rural populations. https://www.census.gov/3

Vaingankar, J. A., Teh, W. L., Roystonn, K., Goh, J., Zhang, Y. J., Satghare, P., Shahwan, S., Chong, S. A., Verma, S., Tan, Z. L., Tay, B., Maniam, Y., & Subramaniam, M. (2021). Roles, facilitators, and challenges of employment support specialists assisting young people with mental health conditions. *Journal of Occupational Rehabilitation, 31*(2), 405–418. https://doi.org/10.1007/s10926-020-09930-x

Vera, E., Carr, A. L., Roche, M. K., & Daskalova, P. (2018). Contextual predictors of vocational hope in ethnic minority, low-income youth. *Professional School Counseling, 21*(1). https://doi.org/10.1177/1096240918761291

Wald, J. (2009). Work limitations in employed persons seeking treatment for chronic posttraumatic stress disorder. *Journal of Traumatic Stress, 22*(4), 312–315. https://doi.org/10.1002/jts.20430

Walker, J. V., & Peterson, G. W. (2012). Career thoughts, indecision, and depression: Implications for mental health assessment in career counseling. *Journal of Career Assessment, 20*(4), 497–506. https://doi.org/10.1177/1069072712450010

Witters, D. (2023, May). U.S. depression rates reach new highs. *Gallup*. Retrieved from https://news.gallup.com/poll/505745/depression-rates-reach-new-highs.aspx

Wood, K. (2023, June 6). All about the new Strong 244 career and interest assessment. *The Myers-Briggs Company Blog*. https://www.themyersbriggs.com/en-US/Connect-With-Us/Blog/2023/June/All-about-the-new-Strong-244-career-and-interest-assessment

Wong, J., Cohn, E. S., Coster, W. J., & Orsmond, G. I. (2020). "Success doesn't happen in a traditional way": Experiences of school personnel who provide employment preparation for youth with autism spectrum disorder. *Research in Autism Spectrum Disorders, 77*, 101631. https://doi.org/10.1016/j.rasd.2020.101631

Wright, G. G., & Chan, C. D. (2022). Applications of intersectionality theory to enhance career development interventions in response to COVID-19. *Professional School Counseling, 26*(1b), https://doi.org/10.1177/2156759X221106807

Wright, S. L., Perrone-McGovern, K. M., Boo, J. N., & White, A. V. (2014). Influential factors in academic and career self-efficacy: Attachment, supports, and career barriers. *Journal of Counseling & Development, 92*, 36–46. https://doi.org/10.1002/j.1556-6676.2014.00128.x

Ye, Y. (2014). Role of career decision-making self-efficacy and risk of career options on career decision-making of Chinese graduates. *Psychological Reports, 114*(2), 625–634. https://doi.org/10.2466/01.17.PR0.114k20w9

Yoon, E., Morgan, M. Jr., & May, V. (2022). Preparing LGBTQ+ students for postsecondary transitions through career development. In E. M. Hines & L. Owens (Eds.), *Equity-based career development and postsecondary transitions: An American imperative* (pp. 301–324). Information Age Publishing.

Zainudin, Z. N., Hassan, S. A., Abu Talib, M., Ahmad, N. A., Yusop, Y. M., & Asri, A. S. (2020). Technology-assisted career counselling: Application, advantages, and challenges as career counselling services and resources. *International Journal of Academic Research in Business and Social Sciences, 10*(11), 67–93. https://doi.org/10.1007/s10775-015-9298-2

Zunker, V. G. (2008). *Career, work, and mental health: Integrating career and personal counseling.* Sage Publications.

Index

Figures and tables are indicated by "f" and "t" following page numbers.

A

Abuse and neglect, history of, 26
ACA. *See* American Counseling Association
ACA Code of Ethics
    on assessment administration, 81
    on confidentiality, 96
    on co-occurring career and mental health concerns, 94
    on diversity, equity, and inclusion, 62
    on scope of practice, 80, 87
Access to services
    differentiated service delivery model and, 84
    in rural areas, 68–69
    scarcity of counseling resources, 63–64
    technology accessibility and, 91, 116
    telehealth for, 96, 115–116
Accountability, 98–99, 99f, 120
Accountability Bridge Model (Astramovich & Coker), 98–99, 99f
accreditation standards, 5, 45, 94. *See also* Council for the Accreditation of Counseling and Related Educational Programs
ACHA (American College Health Association), 20, 21
Active listening, 90–91
ADHD (attention-deficit/hyperactivity disorder), 69–72
Adverse childhood experiences, 26
AERA (American Educational Research Association), 81
Affective arousal, 73
Affective dimensions of career development, 20–23, 33, 49. *See also* Anxiety; Depression; Hope
African American people, 64–66. *See also* Marginalized populations
Agency
    autonomy and, 95, 100
    career development support and, 3–4
    Chaos Theory of Career and, 53
    Cognitive Information Processing Theory and, 50
    marginalized populations and, 62
    Psychology of Working Theory and, 57
Agreeableness, 25–26
ALGBTIC (Association for Lesbian, Gay, Bisexual, and Transgender Issues in Counseling), 67
Alshabani, N., 8
Alternative employment, 28–29, 117–118
American College Health Association (ACHA), 20, 21
American Counseling Association (ACA). *See also* ACA Code of Ethics

151

ethical principles of, 95–96, 102
National Career Development Association (division). *See* National Career Development Association
Standards for Educational and Psychological Testing, 81
training provided by, 119
20/20: A Vision for the Profession of Counseling project, 4
American Educational Research Association (AERA), 81
American Psychological Association, 17, 40
American School Counseling Association (ASCA), 83–84
Anderson, W. P., 83
Anxiety
  affective dimension of career development and, 20–21
  career and work experiences causing, 46
  career decisions and, 3
  Career Thought Inventory and, 33
  career thoughts and, 21, 25
  college students and, 14, 90–91, 101, 122–123
  COVID-19 pandemic and, 16–17
  self-efficacy and, 24
App-based support, 116
Artificial intelligence (AI), 17, 29, 116–117
ASCA (American School Counseling Association), 83–84
ASD (Autism spectrum disorder), 16, 32, 69–72
Assessments, 31–43
  beneficence and, 95
  card sorts, 40
  Career Decision Self-Efficacy Scale, 35
  Career State Inventory, 35–36
  Career Thoughts Inventory, 33–35

college students, communicating results to, 90–91
competence in, 98
Decision Space Worksheet, 39
intake interviews, 38–39
pro tips for providers on, 41
Self-Directed Search, 36–38, 37*f*
service delivery and scope of practice, 80–82
views from the field on, 42–43
Association for Lesbian, Gay, Bisexual, and Transgender Issues in Counseling (ALGBTIC), 67
Astramovich, R. L., 98–99, 99*f*
Attentional control, 21
Attention deficit disorder (ADD), 70
Attention-deficit/hyperactivity disorder (ADHD), 69–72
Authenticity, 64, 76
Autism spectrum disorder (ASD), 16, 32, 69–72
Autonomy, 95, 100, 102

B

Band, Monica P., 27–29
Bandura, A., 35, 47, 50
Beck Depression Inventory, 34
Beck Hopelessness Scale, 34
Beliefs. *See also* Career thoughts; Self-efficacy
  Career Thoughts Inventory and, 35
  cognitive dimensions of career development and, 23–25
  emotions and, 20
  ethical practice and, 99–100
  executive functioning and, 20
  Happenstance Learning Theory and, 54
  neurodivergent individuals and, 72
  Strong Interest Inventory College Profile and, 43

Beneficence, 95, 102
Bennett, Erin, 42–43
Betz, N. E., 24
Bias, self-awareness and, 66
BIPOC (Black, Indigenous, and People of Color) communities, 64–66. *See also* Marginalized populations
Bipolar disorder, 16, 32, 38
Black people, 64–66. *See also* Marginalized populations
Blesso, Anna Clara, 58–60
Body language, 14
Bottleneck hypothesis, 67
Boundaries, remote work and, 28
Brandeis University, 121–123
Brief therapy models, 122
British Journal of Guidance & Counselling, 87–88
Broaching, 75
Bronfenbrenner, U., 69
Bullock-Yowell, E., 37–38
Bullying, 107
Burnout, 28, 75–76
Byars-Winston, A., 72

C

CACREP (Council for the Accreditation of Counseling and Related Educational Programs), 4–5, 32, 82, 94
Calhoun, Brian, 90–91
Capella University, 74–77
Card sorts, 40
Career adaptability, 20, 26, 69
Career and counseling theories, 45–60
    beneficence and, 95
    Career Construction and Life Design frameworks, 52
    Chaos Theory of Career, 52–53
    cognitive theories, 48–51
    defined, 45–46
    dimensions of health, 46–47
    Happenstance Learning Theory, 54–55
    Holland's theory of career choice, 47–48
    Hope-Action Theory, 55, 56*f*
    postmodern approaches, 51
    pro tips for providers on, 57–58
    Psychology of Working Theory, 56–57
    Trait and Factor Theory, 10–11
    views from the field on, 58–60
Career anxiety, 3, 16–17, 21, 25, 46
Career barriers
    group career interventions for, 65–66
    marginalized populations and, 61–77. *See also* Marginalized populations
    self-efficacy and, 24, 51
    socioeconomic status, 57
    women and, 22, 64, 67
Career coaching, 6
Career Construction and Life Design frameworks, 52
Career construction interview (CCI), 52
Career counseling, defined, 6
Career counselors. *See* Providers
Career decision-making readiness
    ASCA National Model and, 83–84
    Career State Inventory and, 35–36
    Cognitive Information Processing Theory and, 49
    defined, 35
    differentiated service delivery model and, 84
    facilitating, 5
    individualized services and, 115
Career Decision Self-Efficacy Scale (CDSES), 35
Career development, 1–14
    in counseling profession, 4–5
    defined, 6
    history of, 7–11, 8–9*t*

mental health and, 15–29. *See also* Career development and mental health
prevention and wellness, 2–4, 3*f*
pro tips for providers on, 11–12
terms, definitions of, 5–6
views from the field on, 12–14
Career development and mental health, 15–29
affective dimensions and, 20–23
assessments and, 31–43. *See also* Assessments
case studies on, 105–112
cognitive dimensions and, 23–25
connection between, evidence of, 18–19
counseling theories and, 45–60. *See also* Career and counseling theories
ethics and, 93–104. *See also* Ethics
executive functioning and, 19–20
familial and personality factors, 25–26
future directions for, 113–124. *See also* Future of integrated career and mental health counseling
integrated assessments, 31–43. *See also* Assessments
marginalized populations and, 61–77. *See also* Marginalized populations
pro tips for providers on, 27
service delivery and scope of practice, 79–91. *See also* Service delivery and scope of practice
societal trends in career development and, 16–17
theory, research, and practice integration, 17–18, 18*f*
trauma and, 26

views from the field on, 27–29
The Career Development Quarterly (journal), 87–88
Career education, 6
Career engagement, 22, 59–60
Career exploration
career thoughts and, 24
depression, effect on, 22
marginalized populations and, 107
mental health support and, 94
purpose in life and, 29
self-efficacy and, 24
trait anxiety and career decision-making, 21
values and, 29
Career Flow, 55
Career-focused events, 97
Career guidance, 6
Career indecision. *See* Decision-making skills
Career narratives, 13–14, 52–53
Career opportunities, 13, 54–55, 87
Career planning services, 6
Career State Inventory (CSI), 35–36, 119
Career thoughts
anxiety and, 21, 25
Career Thoughts Inventory and, 33–35
cognitive dimensions of career development and, 24–25
depression and, 22, 25
hopelessness and, 22
personality factors and, 26
self-efficacy and, 24
Career Thoughts Inventory (CTI), 33–35, 119
Case studies, 105–112
community agencies, 108–109
governmental agencies, 111–112
K-12 schools, 106–108
private practice, 109–111
CASVE (Communication, Analysis, Synthesis, Valuing, and Execution) cycle, 49–50

CBT (cognitive behavioral therapy), 48–49, 50, 102
CCC (Certified Career Counselor), 97
CCI (career construction interview), 52
CDSES (Career Decision Self-Efficacy Scale), 35
Center for Credentialing and Education, 87, 97
Certifications in career development, 87
Certified Career Counselor (CCC), 97
Certified Master of Career Services (CMCS), 97
CFA (Cultural Formulation Approach), 65–66
Chan, C. D., 64, 73
Chaos Theory of Career (CTC), 52–53, 58–60
Child abuse and neglect, 26
Chronic posttraumatic stress disorder (CPTSD), 26
Chronosystems, 69
CIP (cognitive information processing theory), 25, 33, 49–50, 115
Civil Rights Acts of 1965 & 1991, 8
Client safety
    accountability and, 98–99, 99f
    beliefs and values, 99–100
    confidentiality and, 96–97, 102–103, 116
    counselor training and, 97–98
CMCS (Certified Master of Career Services), 97
Codes of ethics. *See* ACA Code of Ethics; NCDA Code of Ethics
Cognitive behavioral therapy (CBT), 48–49, 50, 102
Cognitive beliefs. *See* Beliefs
Cognitive dimensions of career development, 23–25, 33, 49. *See also* Career thoughts; Self-efficacy
Cognitive information processing (CIP) theory, 25, 33, 46, 49–50, 115
Cognitive mapping exercises, 39
Cognitive restructuring, 34–35
Coker, K., 98–99, 99f
Collaborations between providers, 85–86, 95, 103–104, 118–119, 122
College career centers. *See* Views from the field
Community agency settings, 108–109
Competence. *See* Service delivery and scope of practice
Competencies for Counseling (ALGBTIC), 67
Confidentiality, 96–97, 102–103, 116
Conscientiousness, 25–26
Constructivist approach, 40, 52
Contextual messaging, 64
Continuity of care, 82
Coping skills, 23, 48, 64
Cottone, R. R., 46
Council for the Accreditation of Counseling and Related Educational Programs (CACREP), 4–5, 32, 82, 94
Counseling
    career, 15–29. *See also* Career development and mental health
    defined, 4–5
    environments for, 105–112. *See also* Case studies
    ethics and, 93–104. *See also* Ethics
    providers of. *See* Providers
    as scarce resource, 63–64
    theories, 45–60. *See also* Career and counseling theories
Counseling Today (periodical), 88
Counselors. *See* Providers
COVID-19 pandemic
    adaptation to changing environments and, 113
    marginalized populations, impact on, 73
    remote work and, 28, 70

telehealth use and, 115
university students and, 13
work disruptions and, 16–17
CPTSD (chronic posttraumatic stress disorder), 26
Critical consciousness, 56
CSI (Career State Inventory), 35–36, 119
CTC (Chaos Theory of Career), 52–53, 58–60
CTI (Career Thoughts Inventory), 33–35, 119
Cultural Formulation Approach (CFA), 65–66
Cultural identity, 49–50, 65–66, 69, 90
Culturally responsive interventions, 65–66
Cureton, J. L., 23
Currie, J., 26

D

Decent work, defined, 56–57
Decision-making skills
    anxiety and, 21, 122
    BIPOC girls and career barriers, 64
    Career Decision Self-Efficacy Scale, 35
    career development support and, 4
    Career State Inventory and, 35–36
    Career Thoughts Inventory and, 33–34
    depression and, 21–22
    micro-interventions and app-based support for, 116
Decision Space Worksheet (DSW), 39–40
Depression
    affective dimension of career development and, 21–22
    assessments for, 34
    career and work experiences causing, 46
    career development and, 122
    career thoughts and, 22, 25
    Career Thoughts Inventory and, 34
    community agency settings and, 108
    diminished interests and, 38
    prevalence of, 21
    rates of, 110, 114
    referrals for, 13, 85
    work-related difficulty and, 16, 32
Diagnostic and Statistical Manual of Mental Disorders, 5th edition, text revision (DSM-5-TR), 16, 32
Diagnostic process, 16, 32, 38, 82, 83
Dieringer, D. D., 34
Differentiated service delivery model, 84–85
Digital literacy, 116
Disability. *See* People with disabilities
Discrimination. *See also* Marginalized populations; Race and ethnicity
    African American accommodations for, 65
    BIPOC girls and career barriers, 64
    in employment, 8
    K-12 school counseling case study, 107
    LGBTQ people and, 67
    problem-solving and decision-making skills, 50
Discrimination Model of Clinical Supervision (Bernard & Goodyear), 98
Disparate impact, 8
Distance counseling, 96, 115–116
Diversity, equity, and inclusion, 63, 67. *See also* Marginalized populations
Do no harm principle, 95, 102

Drop-in consultations, 97
DSM-5-TR (*Diagnostic and Statistical Manual of Mental Disorders,* 5th edition, text revision), 16, 32
DSW (Decision Space Worksheet), 39–40
Dual relationships, 102
Dysfunctional career thoughts, 25
Dyslexia, 69–72
Dyspraxia, 69–72

E

Eating disorders, 16, 32
Ecological Model (Bronfenbrenner), 69
EMDR (Eye Movement Desensitization and Reprocessing), 109
Emotional intelligence, 20
Emotions. *See also* Anxiety; Depression; Hope
    affective dimensions of career development and, 20–23, 33, 49
    beliefs and, 20
    career thoughts and, 21, 26
    executive functioning and, 20
Employment discrimination, 8
Employment instability
    COVID-19 pandemic and, 16–17
    gig economy and, 28–29, 117–118
    suicide risk and, 23
    unemployment and, 4, 13, 22–23, 70, 117–118
Empowerment, 3–5, 13–14, 43, 54, 71
Environmental influence, 25–26, 28, 69. *See also* Familial influence
Equal treatment under the law, 8
Equity, 62–63, 67. *See also* Marginalized populations
Equity-based Career Development and Postsecondary Transitions:
An American Imperative (Hines & Owens), 64
Ethics, 93–104. *See also* ACA Code of Ethics; NCDA Code of Ethics
    accountability and, 98–99, 99*f*
    on assessment administration and interpretation, 81
    autonomy, 95
    beliefs and values, 99–100
    beneficence, 95
    CACREP standards, 94
    confidentiality and, 96–97
    nonmaleficence, 95
    on professional development, 87
    pro tips for providers on, 100–101
    scope of practice and, 80
    training and, 97–98
    veracity, 96
    views from the field on, 101–104
European Commission, 7
Evaluations of services, 88, 98–99, 99*f*, 119–120
Evidence-informed practice, 2–4, 3*f*, 98
Executive functioning
    career development and mental health, 19–20
    cognitive information processing theory and, 33, 49
    defined, 19
    neurodivergent individuals and, 69–72, 122
Existential therapy approach, 109
Exosystems, 69
Extraversion, 25–26
Eye Movement Desensitization and Reprocessing (EMDR), 109

F

Familial influence
    career anxiety and, 101

career development and mental health, 25–26, 122–123
culturally responsive group career interventions and, 65
in Ecological Model, 69
as help or hinder to career development, 87
intake interviews and, 38–39
marginalized populations and, 67
pressure to support family, 76–77, 110
Psychology of Working Theory and, 56–57
remote work and, 28
support in career decisions, 67, 106, 108
Feelings. *See* Emotions
Fidelity, 102
Five Factor Model of Personality, 25
Flexible thinking, 59–60
Flexible work schedules, 117–118
Flores, L. Y., 65
Florida State University, 42–43
Focus groups, 98
Freelancing, 28–29, 117–118
Future of integrated career and mental health counseling, 113–123
    complex needs and individualized services, 114–115
    intentional collaboration, 118–119
    outcomes measurement, 119
    practitioner-focused research, 119–120
    pro tips for providers on, 120–121
    technology, 115–117
    training, 119
    trends, 117–118
    views from the field on, 121–123

G

GCDF (Global Career Development Facilitator), 97
Gender. *See* Women
Gender identity, 42–43, 66–68
Gender roles, 94
Generation Z, 101
Gibbons, M. M., 69
Gig economy, 28–29, 117–118
Glassdoor, 116
Global Career Development Facilitator (GCDF), 97
Globalization, 94
Goals
    in Career Decision Self-Efficacy Scale, 35
    career development and, 13–14
    career thoughts and, 23–24
    Chaos Theory of Career and, 59
    continued support for achievement of, 123
    culturally driven motivations and, 75
    depression and, 22
    hope and, 22, 55
    neurodivergent individuals and, 72
    Social Cognitive Career Theory and, 50–51
Governmental agency settings, 111–112
Great Recession, 15–16
Group career interventions, 65–66
Guest speakers, 68

H

Hagen, J. W. and W. W., 8
Happenstance Learning Theory (HLT), 54–55
Hayden, S. C. W., 20, 22, 98
Health insurance benefits, 118
Herr, E. L., 5–6
Hines, E. M., 64
History of career development, 7–11, 8–9t

Holland, John, 36, 47–48
Holland Occupational Code (HOC), 36–38, 37f
Holland's RIASEC Hexagon: A paradigm for life and work decisions (Bullock-Yowell & Reardon), 37–38
Hope
    affective dimension of career development and, 22–23
    Beck Hopelessness Scale, 34
    BIPOC people and vocational hope, 65
    Hope-Action Theory, 55, 56f
    Hope-Centered Career Inventory, 55
    hopelessness, 13, 22–23, 34
    neurodivergent individuals and, 71
    SHORES model and, 23
Huston, M., 14, 18–19

I

Identity
    career stress and burnout, 75–76
    cultural, 49–50, 65–66, 69, 90
    diversity, equity, and inclusion, 62
    ethnic identity and racism stress, 65
    intersections of, 62, 72–73
    professional, 72
    sexual, 66–68
    stability of, 67
    student career conversations and, 122
    vocational, 22, 25
Independent contractors, 28–29, 117–118
Indigenous people, 64–66. *See also* Marginalized populations
Individualized services, 102, 114–115
Indivisible Self Evidence-Based Model, 2–4, 3f
Informational interviews, 90
Information processing. *See also* Executive functioning
    cognitive information processing theory, 25, 33, 46, 49–50, 115
    pyramid of information processing, 33, 49
Informed consent, 96–97
Intake interviews, 38–39
Integrated assessments. *See* Assessments
International Association of Vocational Education and Guidance, 119
Interpersonal violence, 26
Intersectionality, 62, 72–73
In-Work Project, 7
Isolation, 13, 26, 28

J

Job search process, 61–62, 65, 70
Journal of Counseling & Development, 87–88
Journal of Employment Counseling, 87–88
Journal of Vocational Behavior, 87–88
Journals, 26–27, 87–88
Justice, 102. *See also* Social justice

K

K-12 school settings, 106–108. *See also* School counselors
Krumboltz, J. D., 47, 54

L

Latina/o people, 64–66. *See also* Marginalized populations
Learning disabilities, 69–72, 122

Leierer, S. J., 119
Lenz, J. G., 97–98
LGBTQ+ populations, 7, 42–43, 66–68, 115. *See also* Marginalized populations
Life Design, 52
Life-Span, Life-Space Theory (Super), 47
LinkedIn, 116
Long-term disability, 16
Luzzo, D. A., 64

M

Macrosystems, 69
Mandated reporting, 102–103
Marginalized populations, 61–77. *See also* Discrimination; Race and ethnicity
    BIPOC communities and, 64–66
    career counseling and social change, 7–8
    counseling as scarce resource for, 63–64
    intersectional identities and career development, 72–73
    LGBTQ populations, 66–68
    neurodivergent individuals, 69–72
    pro tips for providers on, 74
    rural communities, 68–69
    societal trends and employment, 118
    views from the field and, 74–77
McWhirter, E. H., 64
Meaning in Life Questionnaire (MLQ), 34
Mental fatigue, 91
Mental health. *See* Career development and mental health; *specific conditions*
Mentors, 67, 68
Mesosystems, 69
Metacognitive functions, 19, 49
Micro-interventions, 116

Microsystems, 69
Military enlistment and service, 77, 79–80, 111–112, 115
Mindful Healing Counseling Services, LLC, 27–29
Mindfulness, 28
MLQ (Meaning in Life Questionnaire), 34
Monitoring and control, 19, 49
Morgan, Helen, 101–104
Morton, Felix, IV, 74–77
Motivational interviewing, 115
Murray, C. E., 17
Myers-Briggs Company, 43

N

Narrative realities, 13–14, 52
National Assessment of Educational Progress (NAEP), 68
National Career Development Association (NCDA) [ACA division]. *See also* NCDA Code of Ethics
    certifications in career development, 54
    history of, 4
    networking through, 62
    non-degree members of, 96–97
    training provided by, 97, 119
National College Health Assessment (ACHA), 20, 21
National Council on Measurement in Education (NCME), 81
Nation's Report Card (NAEP), 68
Native Americans, 64–66. *See also* Marginalized populations
NCDA Code of Ethics
    on assessment administration, 81
    on confidentiality, 96
    on co-occurring career and mental health concerns, 94
    on diagnosing, 83
    on diversity, equity, and inclusion, 62

on evidence-informed practice, 98
on scope of practice, 87
NCME (National Council on Measurement in Education), 81
Networking, 13, 62, 102
Neurodivergence, 69–72, 122. *See also* Marginalized populations
Neuroticism, 25–26
Niles, S. G., 83
Nilsson, J. E., 67
Non-licensed career services, 96–97, 102
Nonmaleficence, 95, 102
Nudges, 116

O

Objective assessments
    Career Decision Self-Efficacy Scale, 33–35
    Career State Inventory, 35–36
    Career Thoughts Inventory, 33–35
    Self-Directed Search, 36–38, 37*f*
Occupational Alternatives Questionnaire, 36
Online applications, 116
Openness, 25–26
Oppression, 62, 72–73, 77. *See also* Marginalized populations
Outcome evaluations, 88, 98–99, 99*f*, 119–120
Outcome expectations, 50–51
Owens, L., 64

P

Parental influence. *See* Familial influence
Parsons, Frank, 2, 7, 9–11, 47, 48
Penn State Worry Questionnaire (Molina & Borkovec), 119
People with disabilities, 16, 69–72, 122. *See also* Marginalized populations
Personality factors
    career and counseling theories, 48
    career development and mental health, 25–26
    Psychology of Working Theory and, 56
    RIASEC model of personality types, 36–38, 37*f*, 48
Person-centered therapy, 102, 114–115
Pesce, N. L., 70
Peterson, G. W., 22
Pope, Mark, 7–8
Postmodern counseling theories, 51
Posttraumatic growth, 26
Posttraumatic stress disorder (PTSD), 26, 112
Poverty. *See* Socioeconomic status
Practitioner-focused research, 119–120
Privacy, 96–97, 102, 116
Private practice settings, 109–111
Problem-solving skills
    anxiety and, 21
    career decision-making readiness and, 35–36
    career development support and, 4
    Career Thoughts Inventory and, 33–34
    Chaos Theory of Career and, 52–53
    Cognitive Information Processing Theory and, 49
    executive functioning and, 19–20
    hope and, 22
    Life Design and, 52
    micro-interventions and app-based support, 116
Professional development, 87–88, 97, 119, 122. *See also* Training
Professional identity, 72
Professional liability, 97–98

Professional literature, 26–27, 87–88
Professional organizations, 62. *See also specific organizations*
Program evaluation, 119–120
Pro tips for providers
　on assessments, 41
　on career and counseling theories, 57–58
　on career development and mental health, 27
　on career development relevance, 11–12
　on ethics, 100–101
　on future of integrated career and mental health counseling, 120–121
　on marginalized populations, 74
　on service delivery and scope of practice, 89
Providers
　collaborations among, 85–86, 95, 103–104, 118–119, 122
　perspectives. *See* Views from the field
　practitioner-focused research, 119–120
　professional development for, 87–88, 97, 119, 122. *See also* Training
　service delivery and scope of practice, 79–91. *See also* Service delivery and scope of practice
　tips for. *See* Pro tips for providers
　views from the field of. *See* Views from the field
Psychiatric disorders, 16, 32
Psychological testing, 31
Psychology of Working Theory (PWT), 56–57
PTSD (posttraumatic stress disorder), 26, 112
Purpose in life
　career exploration and, 29
　depression and, 22
　Meaning in Life Questionnaire, 34
　SHORES model and, 23
Pyramid of information processing, 33, 49

R

Race and ethnicity. *See also* Discrimination; Marginalized populations
　career counseling, impact for, 8
　K-12 school counseling case study, 106–108
　occupational access and attainment, 7
　stress based on, 65
　suicidal ideation and, 114
Readiness. *See* Career decision-making readiness
Reardon, R. C., 37–38
Reauthoring, 13–14, 52
Redekopp, D. E., 14, 18–19
Referrals, 1, 13, 85, 95, 103
Relational-cultural theory, 64
Remote work, 28, 70, 117
Research
　accountability in, 98–99
　focus groups for, 98
　gap between practice and, 17
　journals on career development and mental health, 26–27, 87–88
　practitioner-focused, 119–120
　single-subject research design, 98, 120
　theory and practice, integration of, 17–18, 18*f*
Resilience, 72
RIASEC model of personality types, 36–38, 37*f*, 48
Rogers, J. G., 72
Role models, 68
Role plays, 28

Rottinghaus, P. J., 22
Rural communities, 68–69, 109–110. *See also* Marginalized populations

S

Sampson, J. P., 17–18, 18*f*, 19, 63
Saunders, D. E., 22
Savickas, M. L., 5
SCCT (Social Cognitive Career Theory), 24, 35, 46, 50–51, 72
Schizophrenia, 16, 32
Schlesinger, Jon, 121–123
Schmidt, C. K., 67
School counselors
    Career Thoughts Inventory and, 34
    education on career development, 5
    K-12 schools case study, 106–108
    marginalized populations and, 68
    scope of practice, 83–84
Scope of practice. *See* Service delivery and scope of practice
SDS (Self-Directed Search), 36–38, 37*f*, 119
Self-awareness, 19, 49, 59, 66
Self-blame, 57
Self-concept, 47, 51, 52, 66
Self-determination, 69. *See also* Agency
Self-Directed Search (SDS), 36–38, 37*f*, 119
Self-efficacy
    BIPOC communities and, 64
    career counseling and, 23
    Career Decision Self-Efficacy Scale, 35
    career development and, 13–14
    cognitive dimension of career development and, 23–24
    defined, 23–24
    dysfunctional career thoughts and, 25
    familial influence and, 25
    hope and, 22
    intersectionality and, 73
    Social Cognitive Career Theory and, 50–51
    student career conversations and, 123
Self-esteem, 35, 67, 101
Self-harm, 23, 102–103, 114
Self-talk, 19, 49
Service delivery and scope of practice, 79–91. *See also* Training
    assessment, 80–82
    differentiated service delivery model, 84–85
    nonmaleficence and, 95
    practice, 82–84
    pro tips for providers on, 89
    provider collaborations, 85–86
    recommendations for integration of, 87–88
    referrals, 1, 13, 85, 95, 103
    veracity and, 96
    views from the field, 90–91
Session Rating Scale (Duncan), 119
Sexual assault, 111–112
Sexual identity. *See* LGBTQ+ populations
SHORES model (Cureton & Tovey), 23
SII (Strong Interest Inventory College Profile), 42–43
Siloed services, 85, 89
Single-subject research design, 98, 120
Smartphone use, 116
Social Cognitive Career Theory (SCCT), 24, 35, 46, 50–51, 72
Social integration, 7
Social justice, 10, 62, 63–64. *See also* Marginalized populations
Social learning theory (Bandura), 35, 47, 50
Social learning theory of career counseling (Krumboltz), 47

Socially persuasive communication, 73
Social media, 29, 102, 116
Social skills, 71
Social support, 24, 56, 71
Social Transition State Model (Pope), 7–8
Societal trends in career development, 16–17. See also Technology
Society of Vocational Psychology, 119
Socioeconomic status
    BIPOC people and vocational hope, 65
    career barriers, 57
    decision-making and problem-solving, impact on, 49–50
    Great Recession and, 16
    as help or hinder to career development, 87
    mental health support and, 94
    Psychology of Working Theory and, 56–57
    rural communities and, 68
Soto, S., 8
Spiritual affiliations, 49–50
Standards for Educational and Psychological Testing (AERA, APA, & NCME), 81
State anxiety, 21
STEM fields, 68
Stereotypes, 66. See also Marginalized populations
Stoltz, K. B., 69
Story Wheels, 55
Stress. See also Anxiety
    artificial intelligence and, 117
    burnout and, 75–76
    family, providing for, 76–77
    neurodivergence and, 71
    posttraumatic stress disorder, 26, 112
    racism and, 65
Strong 244 Career & Interest Assessment, 43
Strong Interest Inventory College Profile (SII), 42–43
Subjective assessments, 38–40
Substance use issues, 114
Suicide and suicidal ideation, 23, 102–103, 114
Super, D. E., 47
Supervision, 97–98

T

Taylor, K. M., 24
Technology
    accessibility to, 91, 116
    artificial intelligence and, 17, 29, 116–117
    assistive and app-based mental health support, 29, 116
    distance counseling and, 96, 115–116
    future of integrated career and mental health counseling, 115–117
Telehealth, 96, 115–116
Theory, Research, Practice Cycle (Sampson), 17–18, 18*f*
Theory of Types and Person-Environment Interactions (Holland), 47–48
Therapeutic relationships, 102–103
Thoughts. See also Beliefs; Career thoughts
    cognitive dimensions of career development and, 23–25
    emotions and, 21
    executive functioning and, 20
    self-talk, 19, 49
Time management skills, 26, 28
Title IX, 102
Tovey, B., 23
Training. See also Professional development
    in assessment instruments, 81–82
    on broaching skills, 75

in career counseling, 2, 4–5, 15, 45–46
in ethical practice, 97–98
rural practitioners and, 68
for school counselors, 5
service delivery and scope of practice, 79–91. *See also* Service delivery and scope of practice
staff onboarding and, 121–122
staying current on future trends, 119
Trait and Factor Theory (Parsons), 10–11
Trait anxiety, 21
Transgender clients. *See* LGBTQ+ populations
Trauma
  adverse childhood experiences, 26
  career development and, 26
  EMDR for, 109
  impact on mental health, 115
  intersectionality and, 72
  posttraumatic stress disorder, 26, 112
  referral for, 85
  sexual assault and, 111–112
  veterans and, 79–80
Trends. *See* Future of integrated career and mental health counseling
True reasoning, 48
Trust, 102–103
Truthfulness, 96
20/20: A Vision for the Profession of Counseling project, 4

U

Underserved communities, 68–69. *See also* Marginalized populations
Unemployment, 4, 13, 22–23, 70, 117–118
University career centers. *See* Views from the field
University of Connecticut School of Business, 58–60
University of Virginia, 15–16

V

Values. *See also* Familial influence
  card sorts and, 40
  career exploration and, 29, 32
  ethical practice and, 99–100
  hope and, 22
  identity development and, 65, 122
  marginalized populations and, 65, 69, 74–75
  Psychology of Working Theory and, 56–57
Veracity, 96, 102
Veterans, 79–80. *See also* Military enlistment and service
Veterans Administration, 111–112
Vicarious learning, 73
Views from the field
  on assessments, 42–43
  on career and counseling theories, 58–60
  on career development and mental health, 27–29
  on career development relevance, 12–14
  on ethics, 101–104
  on future of integrated career and mental health counseling, 121–123
  on marginalized populations, 74–77
  on service delivery and scope of practice, 90–91
Vocational Bureau of Boston, 9
Vocational education and guidance, 6
Vocational guidance movement (Parsons), 9–10

Vocational identity, 22, 25
Volition, 62, 95, 100

W

Wake Forest University, 12–14, 90–91, 101–104
Walker, J. V., 22
Walking the problem, 55
Widom, C. S., 26
Willard, Amy, 12–14
Women
    career barriers and, 22, 64, 67
    career counseling, impact for, 8, 114–115
    interpersonal violence and employment, 26
    occupational access and attainment for, 7
    remote work and, 28
Wong, J., 71
Work in America Survey (American Psychological Association), 17
Work–life balance, 28, 76
Workshops, 97
Worry, 21. *See also* Anxiety
Wright, G. G., 73

About the Author

Dr. Seth C. W. Hayden is an associate professor of counseling, coordinator of the clinical mental health program, and associate director of online counseling programs at Wake Forest University. His research focuses on the connection between career development and mental health. In addition, he examines the career and personal development needs of military service members, veterans, and their families.

He is a licensed clinical mental health counselor in North Carolina, a nationally certified counselor, a certified clinical mental health counselor, and an approved clinical supervisor. He has experience providing counseling in community agencies, non-profit, K-12, and higher education settings.

He is a past president of the Military and Government Counseling Association and National Career Development Association, both divisions of the American Counseling Association. He is a co-author of *Group Career Counseling: Practices and Principles (2nd ed.)* and *Career Development for Transitioning Veterans* and co-editor of *Cognitive Information Processing: Career Theory, Research, and Practice*.

Dr. Hayden received bachelor's degrees in psychology and education from the University of Memphis. He also obtained his master's degree in counseling from the University of Memphis and his doctorate in counselor education from the University of Virginia. He is also a senior research associate at the Florida State University Center for the Study of Technology in Counseling and Career Development.

About the Author

www.ingramcontent.com/pod-product-compliance
Ingram Content Group UK Ltd.
Pitfield, Milton Keynes, MK11 3LW, UK
UKHW021846140426
5217IPUK00022B/1621